Ancient Ballads
Traditionally Sung in New England

Ancient Ballads

Traditionally Sung in New England

From the Helen Hartness Flanders Ballad Collection
Middlebury College, Middlebury, Vermont

Compiled and Edited by
HELEN HARTNESS FLANDERS

Correlated with the numbered
Francis James Child Collection

VOLUME IV • Ballads 250–295

Critical Analyses by **Tristram P. Coffin**

Music Annotations by **Bruno Nettl**

Philadelphia · University of Pennsylvania Press

Published in Great Britain, India, and Pakistan
by the Oxford University Press
London, Bombay, and Karachi

Library of Congress Catalogue Card Number: M59–1030

7435
Printed in the United States of America

Contents

5

Contents

Transcribers of Tunes

Transcribers are identified by initial:

M. O.—Marguerite Olney
H. E. F. B.—Elizabeth Flanders Ballard
P. B.—Phillips Barry
G. B.—George Brown
H. H. F.—Helen Hartness Flanders
A. B. L.—Ainslie B. Lawrence

All tunes in Volume IV were transcribed by M. O. except as noted below:

Child Number	Version	Transcriber
250	E	H. E. F. B.
250	F	H. E. F. B.
250	G	H. E. F. B.
250	I	H. E. F. B.
250	K	H. H. F.
250	L	H. E. F. B.
272	A	H. E. F. B.
277	D	G. B.
277	M	G. B.
278	F	H. E. F. B.
278	M	G. B.
278	Q	H. E. F. B.
283	A	H. E. F. B.
283	D	H. E. F. B.
283	E	A. B. L.
283	G	H. E. F. B.
283	K	G. B.

Child Number	Version	Transcriber
283	O	H. E. F. B.
285	B	H. E. F. B.
285	D	H. E. F. B.
285	E	H. E. F. B.
285	F	G. B.
286	E	H. E. F. B.
286	H	H. E. F. B.
286	Q	H. E. F. B.
286	V	H. E. F. B.
286	X	H. E. F. B.
286	Y	H. E. F. B.
286	BB (2d tune)	P. B.
286	EE	H. E. F. B.
286	HH	P. B.
289	D	H. E. F. B.
289	E	P. B.
295	C	P. B.

Abbreviations Used
in the Headnotes to the Ballads

Books

Aarne-Thompson: Aarne, Antti and Thompson, Stith.
Types of the Folk-Tale (Folklore Fellows Communications 74, Helsinki, 1928).

Barry: Barry, Phillips and others. *British Ballads from Maine* (New Haven, 1929).

Belden: Belden, H. M. *Ballads and Songs Collected by the Missouri Folklore Society* (University of Missouri Studies, XV, Columbia, Mo., 1940).

Boggs: Boggs, Ralph. *Index of Spanish Tales* (Folklore Fellows Communications 90, Helsinki, 1930).

Child: Child, Francis J. *The English and Scottish Popular Ballads* (5 vols.; Boston, 1882–1898).

Coffin: Coffin, Tristram P. *The British Traditional Ballad in North America* (Philadelphia, 1950).

Dean-Smith: Dean-Smith, Margaret. *A Guide to English Folk Song Collections, 1822–1952* (Liverpool, 1954).

Greig and Keith: Greig, Gavin and Keith, Alexander. *Last Leaves of Traditional Ballads, etc.* (Aberdeen, 1925).

Laws, *ABBB*: Laws, G. Malcolm. *American Balladry from British Broadsides* (Philadelphia, 1957).

Ord: Ord, John. *The Bothy Songs and Ballads of Aberdeen, Banff, and Moray, etc.* (Paisley, 1930).

9

Periodicals

BFSSNE: Bulletin of the Folk-Song Society of the Northeast, I–XII (Cambridge, Mass., 1930–37).

FFC: Folklore Fellows Communications (Helsinki, 1922——).

HFQ: Hoosier Folklore Quarterly (Bloomington, Indiana, 1942–50).

JAF: Journal of American Folklore (Philadelphia, 1888——).

JFSS: Journal of the Folk-Song Society (London, 1899–1936).

MLN: Modern Language Notes (Baltimore, 1886——).

NYFQ: New York Folklore Quarterly (Ithaca, New York, 1945——).

PMLA: Publications of the Modern Language Association (Baltimore, 1886——).

SFQ: Southern Folklore Quarterly (Gainesville, Florida, 1937——).

WF: Western Folklore (Berkeley, California, 1942——).

Other books are given with complete title, date, and place of publication, and other pertinent information when mentioned in the headnotes. References to previous publications by Mrs. Flanders are given by the title of the book.

Ballads Migrant in New England (with M. Olney [New York, 1953]).

Country Songs of Vermont (with H. Norfleet [New York, 1937]).

A Garland of Green Mountain Song (with H. Norfleet [Boston, 1934]).

The New Green Mountain Songster (with E. Ballard, P. Barry, and G. Brown [New Haven, 1939]).

Vermont Folk-Songs & Ballads (with G. Brown [Brattleboro, Vt., 1931]).

Abbreviations Used to Refer to Tune Collections in the Musical Annotations

AA   Arnold, Byron, *Folksongs of Alabama* (University, Alabama: University of Alabama Press, 1950).

BC1   Bronson, Bertrand Harris, *The Traditional Tunes of the Child Ballads* (Princeton, N.J.: Princeton University Press, 1959) Vol. I.

BES   Barry, Eckstorm, and Smyth, *British Ballads from Maine* (New Haven: Yale University Press, 1929).

BF   Barry, Phillips, *Folk Music in America* (New York: National Service Bureau, 1939).

BI   Brewster, Paul G., *Ballads and Songs of Indiana* (Bloomington: Indiana University, 1940).

BM   Belden, Henry M., *Ballads and Songs Collected by the Missouri Folk-Lore Society* (Columbia: University of Missouri, 1940).

BP   Bayard, Samuel P., "The British Folk Tradition" in George Korson (ed.), *Pennsylvania Songs and Legends* (Philadelphia: University of Pennsylvania Press, 1949).

CNS   Creighton, Helen, *Songs and Ballads from Nova Scotia* (Toronto: J. M. Dent & Sons, 1932).

CS   Cox, John Harrington, *Folk-Songs of the South* (Cambridge: Harvard University Press, 1925).

CWV   Cox, John Harrington, *Folk-Songs mainly from West Virginia* (New York: National Service Bureau, 1939).

DV   Davis, Arthur Kyle, *Traditional Ballads of Virginia* (Cambridge: Harvard University Press, 1929).

EO   Eddy, Mary Olive, *Ballads and Songs from Ohio* (New York: J. J. Augustin, 1939).

FCB4   *The Frank C. Brown Collection of North Carolina Folklore,* Vol. IV, "The Music of the Ballads" (ed.) Jan P. Schinhan (Durham, N.C.; Duke University Press, 1958).

GCM   Gardner, Emelyn E. and Chickering, Geraldine J., *Ballads and Songs of Southern Michigan* (Ann Arbor: University of Michigan Press, 1939).

GN   Greenleaf, Elisabeth B. (ed.), *Ballads and Songs of Newfoundland* (Cambridge. Harvard University Press, 1933).

LNE   Linscott, Eloise H., *Folk Songs of Old New England* (New York: Macmillan, 1939).

MF   Morris, Alton C., *Folksongs of Florida* (Gainesville: University of Florida Press, 1950).

MK   McGill, Josephine, *Folk Songs of the Kentucky Mountains* (New York: Bossey, 1917).

RO1   Randolph, Vance, *Ozark Folksongs,* Vol. I (Columbia; The State Historical Society of Missouri, 1946–1950).

SAA   Smith, Reed, *American Anthology of Old World Ballads* (New York: J. Fisher & Bro., 1937).

Sharp 1 Sharp, Cecil James, *English Folk Songs from the Southern Appalachians,* Vol. I (2nd and enlarged edition; London, New York: Oxford University Press, 1952).

SSC   Smith, Reed, *South Carolina Ballads* (Cambridge: Harvard University Press, 1928).

WBT   Wells, Evelyn K., *The Ballad Tree* (New York: Ronald Press Co., 1950).

Child Ballads 13, 14 C, 45 B^3, 53 F, 79 A, 105 A, 140 A^2, and 278 L are to be found on the long-playing record, New England Folksong Series No. 1, issued and distributed by Middlebury College.

Ancient Ballads
Traditionally Sung in New England

Sir Andrew Barton

(Child 167, but including Henry Martyn, Child 250)

Child, with some hesitation, separated the traditions of "Sir Andrew Barton" (167) and "Henry Martyn" (250). Phillips Barry, *British Ballads from Maine*, 253–8, argues quite convincingly that the two songs should be thought of as one. To Barry, "Henry Martyn" texts are but fragments of "Sir Andrew Barton" in which the chase and capture are omitted. "Sir Andrew Barton" is the older, more complete tale and may end with a hanging or, because of contact with Child 287, "Captain Ward and the Rainbow," with the escape of the pirate. To complicate matters, "Henry Martyn" versions are easily confused and frequently intermix, with the result that a body of Anglo–American songs tell the famous story—some concluding it one way, some another. In this anthology, all the versions—ten of "Sir Andrew Barton" with the hanging, one of "Sir Andrew Barton" with the escape, and one of "Henry Martyn" with no chase and what appears to be an escape—are given under Child 250.

From historical accounts one can learn the true story behind the ballad. A Scot named John Barton was captured by the Portuguese in 1474. The King of Scotland gave Barton's three sons letters of reprisal against Portugal, and the young men went to sea to take advantage of them. However, the young Bartons interpreted their letters so freely that they had soon become outright pirates, preying on the

15

shipping of all nations including that of England. Andrew Barton evidently was the most daring of the group, for Henry VIII finally was forced to send Sir Thomas and Sir Edward Howard to eliminate him. The Howards were successful, Barton was slain in battle, and Henry defended himself to the Scottish throne on the grounds that the victim was a pirate.

In England, Charles Howard, a sixteenth-century Lord Admiral of the Fleet, replaced Sir Thomas and Sir Edward as the defender of English shipping. In America, Charles Stewart, a hero of the Barbary pirate wars and of the War of 1812, succeeded to the role. Barry, *op. cit.*, 256–7, who first identified the Stewart (Stuart, Storrs) of the American texts, discusses the latter substitution in light of pre-convention campaigning by the Pennsylvania Democrats in 1844.

The Flanders texts are quite representative of the forms the ballad takes in both Britain and America. Versions like A–J, with the chase, the hanging, and the stanza concerning "brass and steel" borrowed from "Captain Ward and the Rainbow," are widely found in the States. K, which is close to Barry's A version of 167 and to Child's E version of 250 (from South Carolina), ends with Barton's telling King Henry or King George that "if he reigns upon dry land . . . I reign on the sea." And L, like Child 250A, from Devon, England, names the pirate Henry Martyn, ends with the sinking of the merchantman, and omits the chase. Child would have listed Flanders A–J as 167, K and L as 250.

Besides Barry's remarks mentioned above, consult Child, III, 334 f.; IV, 393 f., and Coffin, 113–114 for discussion. Coffin, 113–114, gives American bibliography for "Henry Martyn" and "Sir Andrew Barton" together. For English references, and they will all be to "Henry Martyn" forms, see Dean–Smith, 72–3, and Belden, 87–8.

All of the tunes for Child 250 are related, with the possible exception of the Brackett tune. The large group can be divided into sub-groups as follows: (1) Bellows, Hayes, Moses; (2) Degreenia, Delorme, Pease; (3) Cassidy; (4) Kneeland; (5) Williams. There is a dearth of tunes for this ballad in the standard literature, and especially of related tunes. The following tunes show general relationship to the large group in this collection: EO p. 78; p. 80; SSC p. 156.

A

About "Andrew Bordeen" Mrs. Silence Buck Bellows writes the following information in letters dated October 13, 1943, and July 24, 1953:

Some years ago, although we already knew it by heart, we asked our father to sing it carefully to us, and we wrote the words for preservation. I thought you might be interested in having a copy, which I am sending herewith. . . . Yes, my father's (Oscar A. Buck) version of it is definitely out of New England. His father, who sang it to him, was born in Massachusetts. My own father was born in western New York State, where I myself was born. But my father's grandfather migrated to New York from Massachusetts early in the nineteenth century, bringing with him his wife and their children, all of the latter quite small, I believe. My grandfather told my father that *his* father used to sing it to him. So you see it was handed down in a New England family. My grandfather's name was Martin Buck, descended from Isaac Buck, who came to Massachusetts from England in the 1630's. Even if, at some early point in its American career, the song had been passed down through the maternal side, it would still be New England, because all the branches that came into our Buck family were definitely New England—the

Russells, Winslows, Fennos, and Whartons. Our version of the song *has* to be New England, and, of course, further back, from England.

H. H. F., Collector
October 13, 1943

Structure: A B C D C D (2,2,2,2,2,2); Rhythm B; Contour; undulating; Scale: hexachordal

t.c. B flat. Note the 9/8 measure before the end and the small range (major sixth).

For mel. rel. see GCM, 213.

Andrew Bordeen

Andrew Bordeen

There were three brothers in merry Scotland,
Three loving brothers were they,
And for to cast lots they did agree
To go robbing all 'round the salt sea;
And for to cast lots they did agree
To go robbing all 'round the salt sea.

The lot it fell on Andrew Bordeen,
The youngest of the three,
And for to maintain the other two,
He went robbing all 'round the salt sea;
And for to maintain the other two,
He went robbing all 'round the salt sea.

They had not sailed three long winter nights
Before a ship they espied,
A-sailing far off and a-sailing far off,
And at length she came sailing close by;
A-sailing far off and a-sailing far off,
And at length she came sailing close by.

"Who's there? Who's there?" cries Andrew Bordeen.
"Who's there that sails so nigh?"
"'Tis we, the rich merchants of merry England;
If there's no offense, let us pass by."
'Tis we, the rich merchants of merry England;
If there's no offense, let us pass by."

"Oh, no, oh, no," cries Andrew Bordeen.
"Oh, no, that ne'er shall be.
I'll have your ship and your cargo boys,
And your bodies I'll drown in the sea;
I'll have your ship and your cargo boys,
And your bodies I'll drown in the sea."

The news it came to King Henery,
The king that wore the crown.
The ship it was taken, the cargo boys,
The merrymen they were all drowned.
The ship it was taken, the cargo boys,
The merrymen they were all drowned.

"Go build a ship," says King Henery,
"And build it strong and sure,
And if Andrew Bordeen ye do not bring in,
My life shall no longer endure.
And if Andrew Bordeen ye do not bring in,
My life shall no longer endure."

The ship was built without delay,
As I do understand,
And Captain Charles Stuart was placed therein,
For to give the bold command;
And Captain Charles Stuart was placed therein,
For to give the bold command.

They had not sailed three long winter nights
Before a ship they espied,
A-sailing far off and a-sailing far off,
And at length she came sailing close by;
A-sailing far off and a-sailing far off,
And at length she came sailing close by.

"Who's there? Who's there?" cries Captain Charles Stuart.
"Who's there that sails so nigh?"
" 'Tis we, the bold robbers of merry Scotland;
If there's no offense, let us pass by.
'Tis we, the bold robbers of merry Scotland;
If there's no offense, let us pass by."

"Oh, no, oh, no," cries Captain Charles Stuart.
"Oh, no, that ne'er shall be.

I'll have your ship and your cargo boys,
And your bodies I'll carry with me.
I'll have your ship and your cargo boys,
And your bodies I'll carry with me."

"Come on! Come on!" cries Andrew Bordeen.
"I care for ye not one pin.
For though ye are lined with cork without,
We are cork and steel within;
For though ye are lined with cork without,
We are cork and steel within."

"Broadsides! Broadsides!" they cried aloud.
The cannon loud did roar.
And Captain Charles Stuart took Andrew Bordeen;
He carried him to far England's shore.
And Captain Charles Stuart took Andrew Bordeen;
He carried him to far England's shore.

"Good news! Good news!" cries King Henery.
"Good news ye bring to me.
'Tis Andrew Bordeen shall be hanged this day,
And all of his company.
'Tis Andrew Bordeen shall be hanged this day,
And all of his company."

B

Sung by Oscar Degreenia of West Cornwall, Connecticut, to H. H. F. and Mrs. H. S. Beal, as sung by his parents to their eight children, living in a log cabin in Barton, Vermont. Mr. Degreenia has lived the last seventeen years in West Cornwall. Published in Ballads Migrant in New England, *201.*

H. H. F., Collector
May 16, 1949

Structure: A B C D (4,4,4,4); Rhythm B; Contour: arc;
Scale: hexachordal

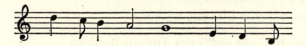

t.c. G flat.

Andrew Batan

Tr. M. O.

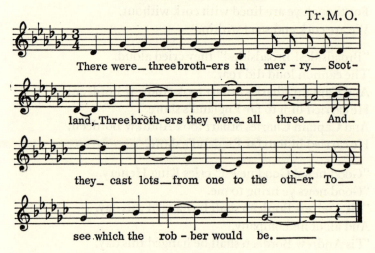

There were three broth-ers in mer-ry Scot-land, Three broth-ers they were all three And they cast lots from one to the oth-er To see which the rob-ber would be.

Andrew Batan

There were three brothers in merry Scotland,
Three brothers they were all three
And they cast lots from one to the other
To see which the robber would be.

The lot did fall on Andrew Batan,
The youngest of the three,
That he would go robbing all on the high sea
To maintain his two brothers and he.

As he was sailing one cold winter's night
A light did soon appear.

They saw a ship sailing far off and far off
And at length it came sailing near.

"Who art, who art," cried Capting Charles Stewart,
"Who art that's sailing so nigh?"
"We art the bold robbers from fair Scotland.
Will you please for to let us pass by?"

"Oh, no, oh, no, that thing we never shall do,
That thing we never shall do.
Your ship and your cargo we'll all take away
And salt water your bodies shall see.
Your ship and your cargo we'll all take away
And salt water your bodies shall see."

The news soon came on England's home shore—
King George he wore the crown—
That the rich merchant's goods had been taken away
And the crew and the captain was drowned,
That the rich merchant's goods had been taken away
And the crew and the captain was drowned.

"Go and build me a ship," cries Captain Charles Stewart;
"Go and build it safe and sure;
I'll take the command from Andrew Batan
Or my life I will never endure."

As he was sailing one cold winter's night
A light did soon appear.
They saw a ship sailing far off and far off
And at length it came sailing near.

"Who art, who art?" cries Captain Charles Stewart;
"Who art, that's sailing so nigh?"
"We are the bold robbers from fair Scotland,
Will you please for to let us pass by?"

"Oh, no, oh, no, that thing we never shall do;
That thing we never shall do.

Your ship and your cargo we'll all take away
And your bodies fair England will see."

"Come on, come on," cried Andrew Batan,
"We fear you not one pin
For we're brass without that makes the fine show
But we are all steel within."

Broadsides, broadsides they quickly put on
And cannons loud did roar
And Capting Charles Stewart took Andrew Batan
And they hung him on England's own shore.

C

*Sung by Hanford Hayes in Stacyville, Maine, to H. H. F.
and Mrs. H. S. Beal, as learned "in the woods." Published
in Ballads Migrant in New England, 72.*

> *H. H. F., Collector*
> *September 22, 1940*

Structure: A B C D C D (4,4,4,4,4,4); Rhythm B; Contour:
pendulum-like; Scale: major, with occasional lowered seventh

t.c. G.

For mel. rel. see GCM, 213.

Andrew Marteen

Tr. M. O.

In bone-y Scot-land three broth-ers did dwell, Three

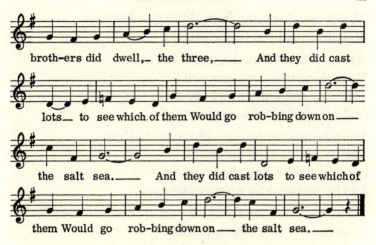

Andrew Marteen

In bone-y Scotland three brothers did dwell,
Three brothers did dwell, the three,
And they did cast lots to see which of them
Would go robbing down on the salt sea.
And they did cast lots to see which of them
Would go robbing down on the salt sea.

The lots they fell on Andrew, fourteen,
The youngest of those brothers three,
That he should go robbing down on the salt sea
To maintain his two brothers and he.
That he should go robbing down on the salt sea
To maintain his two brothers and he.

As he was a-sailing one fine summer's morning
Just as the day did appear,
He spied a large vessel a-sailing far off
And at last she came sailing quite near.

"Art thou, art thou?" cried Andrew Marteen,
"Art thou, a-sailing so high?"

"A rich merchant-ship from old England's shores
And please will you let me pass by?"

"Oh, no, oh, no," cried Andrew Marteen,
"It's a thing that can't very well be;
Your ship and your cargo I will take away,
And your body feed to the salt sea."

The news it went back to old England's shore.
King Henry he wore the crown.
His ship and his cargo were all cast away
And his mariners they were all drowned.

"Come build me a boat," cried Captain Charles Stewart,
"And build it both safe and secure,
And if I don't bring in that Andrew Marteen,
My life I will never endure.
And if I don't bring in that Andrew Marteen,
My life I will never endure."

As he was a-sailing one fine summer's morning,
Just as the day did appear,
He spied a large vessel a-sailing far off,
And at length it came sailing quite near.

"Art thou, art thou?" cried Captain Charles Stewart,
"Art thou a-sailing so high?"
"A Scotch bone-y robber from old Scotland's shore,
And it's please will you let me pass by?"

"Oh, no, oh, no," cried Captain Charles Stewart,
"It's a thing that can't very well be;
Your ship and your cargo I will take away,
And your body feed to the salt sea."

"Fire on, fire on!" cried Andrew Marteen,
"Your talk I don't value one pin.
Your brass at your side makes a very fine show
But I'm pure steel within."

Broadside to broadside those two came together;
Their cannons like thunder did roar,
When Captain Charles Stewart took Andrew, fourteen,
And they hung him on old England's shore.

D

Sung by Mrs. Belle Richards of Colebrook, N. H.

M. Olney, Collector
Sept. 16, 1942

Andrew Bataan

'Twas of three brothers in merry Scotland
And brothers they were all three.
They all did agree to cast lots on each other
And go roving all o'er the salt sea.

The lot it fell on Andrew Bataan,
The youngest of the three;
He was to go roving all o'er the salt sea
To maintain his two brothers and he.

He scarce had sailed one dark cloudy night
Before he saw a light.
He saw a ship sailing far off and far off
And at length it came sailing nigh.

"Who art, who art?" cried Andrew Bataan,
"Who art thou sails so nigh?"
"We are the rich merchants from old England.
Will you please for to let us by?"

"Oh, no, oh, no," cried Andrew Bataan,
"That thing shall never be.
Your ship and your cargo we'll all take away
And your body drown in the salt sea."

The news it reached old England's shore.
King Henry wore the crown.

It grieved him to know that his ship it was lost
And his noblemen they were all drowned.

"Go rig me a ship," cried Captain Charles Storr,
"Go rig it safe and sure
And if Andrew Bataan I do not bring here
My life I will never endure."

They scarce had sailed one dark cloudy night
Before they saw a light.
They saw a ship sailing far off and far off
And at length it came sailing nigh.

"Who art, who art," cried Captain Charles Storr,
"Who art thou sails so nigh?"
"We are the Scotch robbers from merry Scotland.
Will you please for to let us pass by?"

"Oh, no, oh, no," cried Captain Charles Storr,
"That thing shall never be.
Your ship and your cargo we'll all take away
And your body old England shall see."

"Come on, come on," cried Andrew Bataan,
"We fear you not one pin,
For brass without will make a fine show
But we're all good steel within."

Broadside to broadside they came sailing up.
The cannons loud did roar,
But Captain Charles Storr took Andrew Bataan;
He was hung on old England's shore.

E

As sung by Jonathan Moses, Orford, New Hampshire

M. Olney, Collector

Structure: A B C D C D (2,2,2,2,2,2); Rhythm B; Contour: arc; Scale: hexachordal

t.c. G.

For mel. rel. see GCM, 213.

Andrew Bateen

Tr. H. E. F. B.

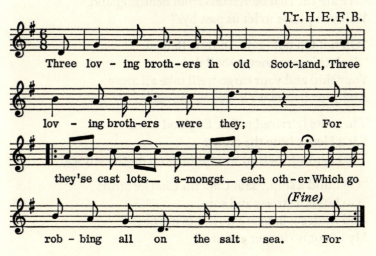

Three lov - ing broth-ers in old Scot-land, Three

lov - ing broth-ers were they; For

they'se cast lots— a-mongst— each oth-er Which go

(Fine)

rob - bing all on the salt sea. For

Andrew Bateen

(Last two lines of each verse repeated, verses 6 and 8 excepted.)

Three loving brothers in old Scotland,
Three loving brothers were they;
For they'se cast lots amongst each other
Which go robbing all on the salt sea.

The lot it fell to Andrew Bateen,
The youngest of all three,

That he should maintain his two brothers and he
By robbing all on the salt sea.

They scarce had sailed one cold winter's night
Until the day appeared;
They spied a ship a-sailing far off and a-sailing far on,
And at length it came sailing near by.

"Who art, who art?" says Andrew Bateen,
"Who art that sails so nigh?"
"We are the rich merchants from near England.
Will you please to let us pass by?"

"Oh no! Oh no!" says Andrew Bateen,
"Such things we never shall do!
Your ship and your cargo we'll take all away
And your bodies we'll feed to the sea."

The news it 'rrived to fair England town—
King Henry bore the crown—
That Andrew Bateen was robbing all on the salt sea.

"Go build a ship," said Captain Charles Storr;
"Go build it strong and sure,
And Andrew Bateen I do not bring back
My life or no longer endure."

They scarce had sailed one cold winter's night
Until the day appeared;
They spied a ship a-sailing far off and a-sailing far on
And at length it came sailing near by.

"Who art, who art?" says Captain Charles Storr,
"Who art that sails so nigh?"
"We are the Scotch robbers from old Scotland.
Will you please to let us pass by?"

"Oh no! Oh no!" says Captain Charles Storr,
"Such things we never shall do!

Your ship and your cargo we'll take all away
And your bodies to fair England shore."

"Come on! Come on!" says Andrew Bateen,
"I fear you not one pin!
For brass without it makes a fine show
But we're all steel within."

Broadside, broadside, oh, then they stood
And the cannons loudly roared;
And Captain Charles Storr took Andrew Bateen
And he carried him to fair England shore.

"Go build a gallus," said Captain Charles Storr,
"Go build it strong and sure,
And Andrew Bateen shall be hung thereon
And the rest of his companee." (*Last word spoken*)

F

Sung by Mrs. Alice Cassidy of East Matunuck, Rhode Island.

M. Olney, Collector
April 5, 1945

Structure: A B C D¹ D² (2,2,3,2,2); Rhythm divergent; Contour: arc-like; Scale: major

t.c. F.

Three Loving Brothers

Tr. H. E. F. B.

In Scot-land were three lov-ing broth-ers, Three
lov - ing broth-ers all three. And

they cast lots to see which one of them Should go

sail-ing down on the salt sea, salt sea,

Should go sail-ing down on the salt sea.

Three Loving Brothers

In Scotland were three loving brothers,
Three loving brothers all three.
And they cast lots to see which one of them
Should go sailing down on the salt sea, salt sea,
Should go sailing down on the salt sea.[1]

The lot did fall to Abner Bardeen,
The younger of these brothers three,
That he should go sailing down on the salt ocean,
To maintain his two brothers and he, and he,
To maintain his two brothers and he.

He had not sailed far one cold frosty morning,
One cold frosty morning in May,
When he espied a rich merchantman,
Sailing down under the lee, his lee,
Sailing down under his lee.

"Who's there? Who's there?" cried Abner Bardeen.
"Who's there, I cried unto thee?" [1]
"A rich merchantman all laden down fine;

[1] In a text sent to Mrs. Flanders on February 12, 1945, Mrs. Cassidy used the word "robbing" instead of "sailing" in Lines 4 and 5 of Stanza 1, and wrote "Who's there, unto thee I cry" for Line 2 of Stanza 4.

Oh, will you please let us pass by, and
Will you please let us pass by?"

"Oh, no, oh, no!" cried Abner Bardeen.
"Oh, no! I cry unto thee,
Since I've taken to robbing down on the salt ocean
To maintain my two brothers and me, and me,
To maintain my two brothers and me.

"So lower your topsail and take your main pack,
And bring your ship under our lee.
I will take your gold, your rich flowing gold,
And your bodies to sink in the sea, salt sea,
And your bodies will sink in the sea."

"We'll not lower our topsail or take our main pack,
Nor bring our ship under your lee.
But we'll fight for our gold, our rich flowing gold,
And our bodies we'll save from the sea, salt sea,
And our bodies we'll save from the sea."

"Broadside! Broadside!" cried Abner Bardeen.
"I cry, I cry unto thee."
At last Abner Bardeen was taken unharmed,
And his body now sleeps in the sea, salt sea,
And his body now sleep in the sea.

G

*The words of this ballad were written down by Mrs. Bertha
J. Kneeland of Searsport, Maine, 1914, from the singing of
her father-in-law, James Henry Kneeland, whose grandfather, Edward Kneeland, came from Boston to Cape Jellison about 1785.*

M. Olney, Collector
June 17, 1941.

Structure: A B C D C D (2,2,2,2,2,2); Rhythm A and B; Conture: arc; Scale: Mixolydian

t.c. C.

Andrew Batting

Tr. H. E. F. B.

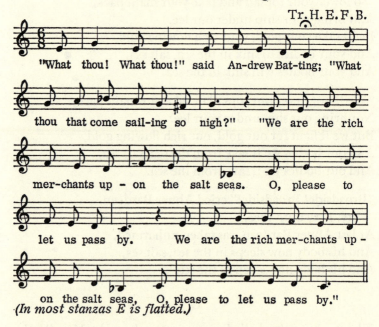

"What thou! What thou!" said An-drew Bat-ting; "What thou that come sail-ing so nigh?" "We are the rich mer-chants up - on the salt seas. O, please to let us pass by. We are the rich mer-chants up - on the salt seas, O, please to let us pass by."

(In most stanzas E is flatted.)

Andrew Batting

"What thou! What thou!" said Andrew Batting;
"What thou that come sailing so nigh?"
"We are the rich merchants upon the salt seas,
O, please to let us pass by—
We are the rich merchants upon the salt seas,
O, please to let us pass by."

"Ah, no! Ah, no!" said Andrew Batting,
"Such a thing there never can be,
Your ship and your cargo we'll both take away,
And your bodies give to the salt sea—
Your ship and your cargo we'll both take away,
And your bodies give to the salt sea."

"Build me a ship," said Captain Charles Stuart,
"And build her strong and sure,
That I may bring in proud Andrew Batting,
Or my life I will never endure—
That I may bring in proud Andrew Batting,
Or my life I will never endure."

We cruis-ed north and we cruis-ed south
For the space of three weeks or more;
At length we spied a ship sailing far off, far off,
And at length she came sailing so nigh—
At length we spied a ship sailing far off, far off,
And at length she came sailing so nigh.

"What thou? What thou?" said Captain Charles Stuart,
"What thou that come sailing so nigh?"
"We are the Scotch pirates upon the salt seas;
O, please to let us pass by—
We are the Scotch pirates upon the salt seas;
O, please to let us pass by."

"Ah, no! Ah, no!" said Captain Charles Stuart,
"Such a thing there never can be;
Your ship and your cargo we'll both take away,
And your bodies give to the salt sea—
Your ship and your cargo we'll both take away,
And your bodies give to the salt sea."

About! About! and they merrily fought
For the space of three hours or more,

At length Captain Charles Stuart took Andrew Batting
And brought him to fair England's shore—
At length Captain Charles Stuart took Andrew Batting
And brought him to fair England's shore.

H

Mailed to H. H. F., January 17, 1945, by Miss Mary Geneva
Rathburn, 35 Denison Avenue, Mystic, Connecticut, who
says it was "sung in 1917 by a resident of Griswold, Con-
necticut, who was born 1824 or 25—learned from his brother
when a small boy." This was previously collected by Miss
Mary Augusta Scott and used in an issue of The Vassar
Quarterly *in 1917.*

H. H. F., Collector
January 17, 1945

Andrew Bardeen

Three brothers, three brothers in Scotland did dwell.
They lived by themselves.
They all cast lots to see which should go robbing,
Go robbing all on the salt sea.

The lot it fell to Andrew Bardeen,
The youngest of the three,
That he should go robbing for the other two,
Go robbing all on the salt sea.

He had scarce sailed two cold winter nights
When he a ship espied
A-sailing far off and a-sailing far off,
And at length it came sailing close by.

"O, who comes there," cries Andrew Bardeen,
"That sails along so nigh?"
"We're the rich merchant vessels from old Scotland.
If there's no offense, let us pass by."

"O no, O no," cries Andrew Bardeen.
"Such things shall never be.
I'll have your ship and your cargo, boys,
And your bodies I'll drown in the sea."

Soon as the news to King Henry came
And noised all around,
That his rich merchant vessels were all taken
And his mariners, they were all drowned,

"Go build me a ship," says King Henry,
"And build it firm and sure.
If Andrew Bardeen I don't fetch o'er,
My life I'll no longer endure."

The ship was built without delay
And ready at his hand.
And Captain Charles Stewart was put therein
To take the bold command.

He had scarce sailed two cold winter nights
When he a ship espied
A-sailing far off and a-sailing far off,
And at length it came sailing close by.

"O who comes there," cries Captain Charles Stewart,
"That sails along so nigh?"
"We are the bold robbers from old Scotland.
If there's no offense, let us pass by."

"O no, O no," cries Captain Charles Stewart.
"Such things can never be.
I'll have your ship and your cargo, too,
And your bodies I'll carry with me."

"Come on, come on," cries Andrew Bardeen;
"Your bodies I don't value one pin,
And though you're made sure with brass without,
I've plenty of steel within."

"Broadsides, broadsides," our captain replied,
And cannon bud [1] did roar,
And Captain Charles Stewart took Andrew Bardeen
And brought him safe to Scotland's shore.

I

As sung by Mrs. Lily M. Delorme of Cadyville, New York, born in Schuyler Falls, New York, in 1869. Mrs. Delorme's father was born in Starksboro, Vermont; her mother in Schuyler Falls. This ballad was learned in her home as a child.

M. Olney, Collector
December 8, 1941

Structure: A¹ A² A³ B (2,2,2,2); Rhythm A; Contour: undulating; Scale: anhemitonic pentatonic

t.c. D.

Andrew Bardeen

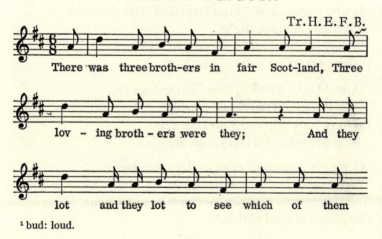

Tr. H. E. F. B.

There was three broth-ers in fair Scot-land, Three

lov - ing broth - ers were they; And they

lot and they lot to see which of them

[1] bud: loud.

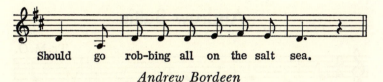

Should   go   rob-bing all   on   the   salt   sea.

Andrew Bordeen

There was three brothers in fair Scotland,
Three loving brothers were they;
And they lot and they lot to see which of them
Should go robbing all on the salt sea.

The lot it fell on Andrew Bordeen,
The youngest brother of three,
That he should go robbing all on the salt sea
To maintain his two brothers all and he.

He had not sailed but leagues two or three,
Before a vessel he saw;
"Who's there, who's there?" cried Andrew Bordeen,
"Who's there come sailing so nigh?"
"We're three merchant ships from old England
And if you please let us pass by."

"Oh, no! Oh, no!" said Andrew Bordeen,
"Oh, no! that never can be;
We'll have your ship and your cargo, too,
And your bodies we'll drown in the sea."

J

As sung by Mrs. Mabel Pease of Orford, New Hampshire.

M. Olney, Collector
November 19, 1942

Structure: A B C D (4,4,4,4); Rhythm B; Contour: undulating; Scale: hexatonic

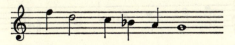

t.c. A.

Andrew Battin

"Rush on, rush on!" cried An-drew Bat - tin. "I
var - y you not a pin!___ Al-though you're lined with
brass with-out I'm a dou-ble steel with - in."___

Andrew Battin

"Rush on, rush on!" cried Andrew Battin.
"I vary you not a pin!
Although you're lined with brass without
I'm a double steel within."

K

*Recorded as sung by Euclid I. Williams, eighty-four years
old, in Lower Waterford, Vt. The last two lines of each verse
are repeated. Printed in* Country Songs of Vermont, 8.

H. H. F., Collector
Summer, 1933

Structure: A B C D C D (2,2,2,2,2,2); Rhythm A; Contour:
undulating; Scale: major, the leading tone appears only at
the end

t.c. E flat.

Andrew Bardeen

Tr. H. H. F.

Three lov-ing broth-ers in Scot-land did dwell   And lov-ing_ were the three.__ They each cast lots to see which of the three Should go rob-bing a-round the salt sea.__ They each cast lots to see which of the three Should go rob-bing a-round the salt sea.__

Andrew Bardeen

Three loving brothers in Scotland did dwell
And loving were the three.
They each cast lots to see which of the three
Should go robbing around the salt sea.

The lot it fell upon Andrew Bardeen,
The youngest of all the three,
And for to maintain his two older brothers
Went robbing around the salt sea.

He had not sailed but one summer night,
When daylight did appear.
He saw a ship sailing very far off
And at last it came sailing quite near.

"Who's there? Who's there?" cried Andrew Bardeen;
"Who's there that sails so nigh?"
"We are the rich merchants from Merrie England
And no offense. Let us by."

"Oh, no, oh, no," said Andrew Bardeen.
"Oh, no, that never can be.
Your ship I'll have and your cargo, too,
And your bodies I'll sink in the sea."

Now when this news reached Merrie England—
King George he wore the crown—
That his ship and his cargo were taken away
And his brave men they were all drowned,

"Go build me a ship," says Captain Charles Stewart,
"A ship both stout and sure,
And if I don't fetch this Andrew Bardeen
My life shall no longer endure."

He had not sailed but one summer's night
When daylight did appear.
He saw a ship sailing very far off;
At last it came sailing quite near.

"Who's there? Who's there?" cried Captain Charles Stewart;
"There that sails so nigh?"
"We are the bold brothers from Merrie Scotland
And no offense. Let us by."

"Oh, no, oh, no," cried Captain Charles Stewart,
"Oh, no, that never can be;
Your ship I'll have and your cargo, too,
And your bodies I'll carry with me."

Then they drew up a full broadside
And each to the other let pour.
They had not fought but a very short time
When Captain Charles Stewart gave o'er.

"Go home, go home," says Andrew Bardeen,
And tell your king for me
That he may reign king of the merrie dry land
But that I will be king of the sea."

L

Sung by Fred Brackett of Stacyville, Maine.

M. Olney, Collector
May 10, 1942

Structure: A B C D (1,1,2,2); Rhythm A but divergent; Contour: arc; Scale: Mixolydian

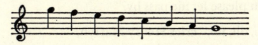

t.c. D Note the irregular meter at the beginning.

Henry Martyn

Tr. H. E. F. B.

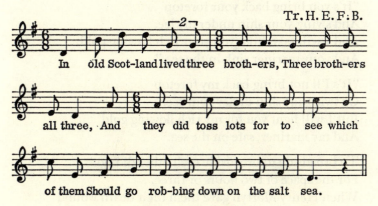

In old Scot-land lived three broth-ers, Three broth-ers all three, And they did toss lots for to see which of them Should go rob-bing down on the salt sea.

Henry Martyn

In old Scotland lived three brothers,
Three brothers all three,
And they did toss lots for to see which of them
Should go robbing down on the salt sea.

The lot it fell to Henry Martyn,
The youngest of the three,
That he should go robbing all on the salt sea,
To maintain his two brothers and he.

He had not been sailing more'n a week or ten days,
A week or ten days or three,
Before he spied a large lofty ship
Come bearing down under his lee.

"Who's there? Who's there?" cried Henry Martyn;
"Who's there that's running so nigh?"
"I'm a rich merchant ship and for fair London bound.
Will you please let me pass by?"

"Oh, no, oh, no," cries Henry Martyn,
"Oh, no, that never can be,
Since I have turned robber all on the salt sea
To maintain my two brothers and me.

"It's you bring back your foretop
And swing your ship under my lee,
And I will take from you your rich flowing gold,
And your mariner sink in the sea."

"It's I'll not bring back my foretop
Or swing my ship under your lee,
But I will fight you for my rich flowing gold
And my mariner, safe on the sea."

To broadside to broadside each other did pour,
For the space of two hours or three,
When Henry Martyn gave them their death wound
And the mariner sank in the sea.

"Bad news, bad news, to old Engaland,
Bad news I will send unto thee,
For I have took from you your rich flowing gold,
And your mariner sank in the sea."

John Thomson and the Turk

(Child 266)

Mrs. Flanders' discovery of "John Thomson and the Turk" is unique in America. The song has not had a wide circulation in oral tradition or in print on either side of the Atlantic, Child having but one full text and one fragment and Dean–Smith not listing it at all. Nevertheless, it tells an old story. Once the tale was associated with King Solomon, although it has spread over most of Europe, and Child, in his headnotes, cites analogues from German poetry, Chrêtian de Troyes, Portuguese legend, Russian narrative, and so forth.

Edwards' text, as most of his unusual ones, is much like Child A. However, there are enough differences to make one feel his family may not have learned the song directly from *The English and Scottish Popular Ballads* or one of the sources. Though incomplete, the Vermont text is more detailed than its counterpart in Child. Edwards' first six stanzas cover what the Child A version covers in three, and Edwards' Stanzas 27–8 cover what Child A includes in Stanza 24. Otherwise, Edwards' Stanzas 7–26, and 29 parallel Child A Stanzas 4–23, and 25 with marked differences in phrasing. The American text breaks off at the point in the story (Child A, Stanza 25) where Thomson tells the Turk he would hang him if their places were to be reversed. Missing is the portion where Thomson signals his men, who come to capture the Turk, burn him in his castle, and hang the false lady in the forest.

45

*Given during an interview, by George Edwards at Burling-
ton, Vermont. This has been handed down in his Northum-
brian family for many generations. Printed in* Ballads Migrant in New England, *91.*

H. H. F., Collector
May 24, 1934

The Trooper and the Turk

John Thomson fought against the Turks,
In a country far away
From Scotland's shore and bonny braes
And from his lady gay.

Three years and more he had been gone
From home, and lady fair;
Now this young chieftain sat alone
His mind on Scotland far.

He thought of his own childhood days,
And the happy hours he spent
When as a youth, o'er moor and fen
His wandering footsteps bent.

It happened once upon a day,
As he was walking down to the sea,
He espied his lady, in rich array,
As she was riding o'er the lea.

"What brought you here, my dear," he said,
"So far from friends and home?
Why did you not let me know that it
Was your desire to come?"

"I pondered long, dear John," she said,
"E'er I made my mind to come;
I longed for your fair face to see;
It was that which lured me from our home."

For some days she did stay with him,
And seemed a loving wife to be,
Then farewell for a time she said
For home again she must away.

He gave her jewels that were rare,
Set with pearls and precious stones,
Saying, "Beware of robbers bold
That are on the way as you go home.

"You'll take the road, my lady fair,
That leads you far across the lea,
That will take you from the Turkish plain
Which is the home of base Vallentree."

These two did part with heavy hearts,
And, as he thought, she was going home;
Instead, she crossed the Turkish plain
And to base Vallentree she's gone.

When a full twelve months had passed,
John Thomson had thought wondrous long;
He wrote a letter to his brother then
And sealed it well with his own hand.

He sent it with a vessel small
That then was quickly going to sea
And sent it on to Scotland fair
And inquired about his gay ladee.

But the answer he received from home
Did grieve his heart right sore;
None of her friends had seen her there
For a year and something more.

Then he put on a palmer's weed
And took a pike-staff in his hand
And to the castle of Vallentree
Slowly his sorrowful way did wend.

And when within the hall he came,
He heavily on his staff did lean;
"If ye be the lady of this hall
Some of your bounty give to me."

"What news, what news, good man," said she,
"And from what country have you come?"
"I'm lately come from Grecian plains
Where camps some of the Scotch army."

"If you be come from Grecian plains
Some other news I'll ask of thee,
Regarding one of the chieftains there.
Has he lately seen his fair ladee?"

"It's a full twelve months and something more,
Since they did part on the Grecian plain;
And now this chieftain has begun to fear
That some of his foes have captured her."

"He has not taken me by force," quoth she;
"It was of my own free will;
He may tarry in the fight
But here I mean to tarry still.

"And if John Thomson you chance to see,
Tell him I wish him very well,
But his wife I can no longer be,
For now I love another man."

He then threw off his strange disguise,
Laid by the mask that he had on,
Saying, "Hide me now, my dearest wife,
For Vallentree will soon be home."

"For the love I bore thee once,
I'll strive to hide you, if I can."
She led him down to the cellar dark,
Where he saw many a newly slain man.

But he had not long in the cellar been
When a sound outside caused him to fear;
It was the tread of many feet
As through the gates came Vallentree.

He greeted her with affection then
And said, "It's time that we should dine;
Bring forth from your most bountiful store,
And serve us with both bread and wine.

"That chief of the Scots, our dreaded foe
Who from the field has made us flee,
Ten thousand guineas in gold I'd give
If I his face were permitted to see."

"If I produce this Scotchman bold
And cause him to before thee stand,
Will you surely keep to me your word
And pay this price into my hand?"

Then from the cellar she brought the chief,
And he came on most dejectedly;
The Turk then paid the price agreed,
And unto the chieftain he did say,

"I have thee in my power now,
And I shall work my will on thee;
But, if things were changed betwixt us both,
What would you do unto me?"

"If I had you, as you have me,
I'll tell you what I would do," he said;
"I would cause your own hand to arrange the tree
And hang you up in yon greenwood."

The Suffolk Miracle

(Child 272)

Child, V, 58 f., indicates that his English text of "The Suffolk Miracle" is not truly a "popular ballad," but that he decided to include it in his collection because it represents a great European story. The tale is known across the Continent, particularly among the Slavs, in a form something like this. Two lovers are separated when the man dies. The girl grieves, and the corpse becomes restless in the grave. The man finally returns from the dead to take his love on a wild night-ride. They end up in the grave, and, even though she finally escapes, she leaves a token, usually a bit of her dress, behind her. The token is discovered later, and before long the girl dies.

In America, the story is much like the one in Child, but usually the death of the girl is omitted. Generally, as Alton Morris pointed out in *SFQ*, VIII, 162, American texts show an improvement in literary style and narrative over Child's version. In this connection see also Phillips Barry's remarks in *BFSSNE*, V, 10.

Flanders A and B are typical, though the ending of A borrowed from "Barbara Allen" (Child 84) is unique. Flanders C, in which the lover seems to have the handkerchief about his head when he arrives at the door, recalls the fragment printed by Phillips Barry, *British Ballads from Maine*, 314. For further American references and discussion, see Coffin, 143–4. The song is not listed in Dean–Smith. Child, V, 58 f., gives a number of European analogues and retells a Cornwall prose version. Schischmanov, *Indegermanische Forschungen* (1894), IV, 412–8, has written an article expounding the thesis that all ballads of "The Dead Brother," as this song is often called, derive from the Greek. Burger's *Lenore* is a famous literary retelling of the story.

The two tunes for Child 272 are related, but not closely.

A

Mrs. Ellen M. Sullivan of Springfield, Vermont, gave these words as sung by her father, Thomas O'Brien, of County Cork, Ireland. Published in The New Green Mountain Songster, *87, and in* BESSNE, *V, 8, with minor variations.*

H. H. F., Collector
July 12, 1932

Structure: A¹ B¹ B² A² (2,2,2,2); Rhythm E; Contour: arc; Scale: hexatonic, but the leading tone appears only at the end

t.c. G.

For mel. rel. see FCB4, 102; MF, 315; Sharp 1, 264 C (distant).

The Suffolk Miracle

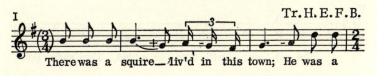

There was a squire__ liv'd in this town; He was a

squire of high re - nown; Had one daugh-ter, a beau - ty

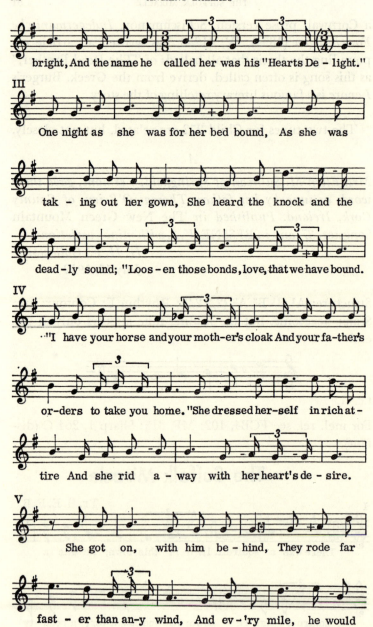

bright, And the name he called her was his "Hearts De – light."

III

One night as she was for her bed bound, As she was

tak – ing out her gown, She heard the knock and the

dead – ly sound; "Loos – en those bonds, love, that we have bound.

IV

·"I have your horse and your moth-er's cloak And your fa-ther's

or-ders to take you home."She dressed her-self in rich at-

tire And she rid a – way with her heart's de – sire.

V

She got on, with him be – hind, They rode far

fast – er than an-y wind, And ev-'ry mile, he would

sigh and say, "O my love-ly jew-el, my head it aches!"

VI
A Hol-land   hand-ker-chief she then took   out

And tied his head with it   a-round;   She kissed his

lips   and she then did   say,   "O my love, you're

cold-er than an-y clay."   When they came to her fa-ther's

gate,   "Come down, dear   jew - el,"   this young man

said,   "Come down, my   dar - ling, and go   to

bed,   And I'll see your horse   in his sta-ble led."

VIII

And when they came to her fa-ther's hall, "Who's there, who's

there?" her fa-ther called; "It is I, dear fa-ther,

did you send for me, By such a mes-sen-ger?" nam-ing

IX

he. Her fa-ther, know.-ing this young man bein'

dead, He tore the grey hair down from his

head; He wrung his hands and he wept full

sore, And this young man's dar-ling cried more and more.

X

The next day to the grave they went, And al-tho' this

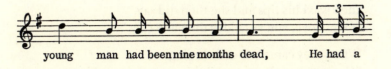

young   man had been nine months dead,   He had a

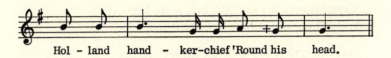

Hol - land   hand - ker-chief 'Round his   head.

The Suffolk Miracle

There was a squire lived in this town;
He was a squire of high renown.
Had one daughter—a beauty bright—
And the name he called her was his "Heart's Delight."

When her father came this to know
He sent his daughter far away,
Sends her over fifty miles or more
To detain her of her wedding day.

One night as she was for her bed bound,
As she was taking out her gown,
She heard the knock and the deadly sound;
"Loosen those bonds, love, that we have bound.

"I have your horse and your mother's cloak
And your father's orders to take you home."
She dressed herself in rich attire
And she rid away with her heart's desire.

She got on, with him behind,
They rode far faster than any wind,
And ev'ry mile he would sigh and say,
"O my lovely jewel, my head it aches."

A Holland handkerchief she then took out
And tied his head with it around.

She kissed his lips and she then did say,
"O my love, you're colder than any clay."

When they came to her father's gate,
"Come down, dear jewel," this young man said,
"Come down, my darling, and go to bed
And I'll see your horse in his stable led."

And when they came to her father's hall,
"Who's there, who's there?" her father called.
"It is I, dear father, did you send for me
By such a messenger?" naming he.

Her father, knowing this young man being dead,
He tore the grey hair down from his head.
He wrung his hands and he wept full sore
And this young man's darling cried more and more.

The next day to the grave they went;
And although this young man had been nine months dead,
He still wore the Holland handkerchief
'Round his head.

The corpse were laid down at her feet.
There she stood a-laughing.
"O fie, for shame," her friends all cried,
"Hard-hearted Barbry Allen!"

"Go make my bed, mama," she said,
"Oh, make it soft and mellow
For a young man died for me last night,
And I'll die for him to-morrow."

"Oh, dig my grave, papa," she said,
"And dig it deep and narrow
For a young man died for me last night
And I'll die for him to-morrow."

One was buried in the middle of the church;
The other, in Mary's Abbey.
Out of one there grew a rose
And out of the other, a briar.

And every night at twelve o'clock
They twined in a true lover's knot
The red rose and the briar.

B

Sung by Hanford Hayes of Stacyville, Maine.

H. H. F., *Collector*
Retake, May 5, 1942

Structure: A¹ B C A² (2,2,2,2); Rhythm E; Contour: arc;
Scale: hexatonic, like the anhemitonic pentatonic, the leading tone appears raised only at the end

t.c. D.

For mel. rel. see DV, 594 No. 42 (B).

The Holland Handkerchief

Tr. M. O.

There was a lord___ lived in this town;

His prais - es went the coun - try 'round;

He had a daugh-ter, a beau-ty bright;

On her he placed____ his heart's de-light.

The Holland Handkerchief

There was a lord lived in this town;
His praises went the country 'round.
He had a daughter, a beauty bright;
On her he placed his heart's delight.

Oh, many a lord a-courting came,
But none of them could her fancy gain,
Till a poor young man of a low degree
Came under hand and she fancied he.

But when her father came this to hear,
He separated her far from her dear.
Four scores of miles he had her sent
To her uncle's house at her discontent.

One night as she was for bed bound
And all things ready for to lie down,
She heard the voice of a deadly sound:
"Unloose those bands that's so costly bound.
Here's your father's orders for to go home."

She dressed herself in quick retire[1]
Her father's steed she quickly knew,
Her mother's mantle and safeguard, too;
And as she mounted on behind,
Rode swifter, faster than the wind.

And all along those words did say,
"My dear and darling, how my head does ache!"
She kissed his lips and those words did say:
"My dear and darling, you're as cold as clay."

Her Holland handkerchief she then pulled out
And bound it 'round his head about,
Saying, "When we get home a good fire we'll have."
But little she knew he came from the grave.

A short while after a little space,
They both arrived at her father's gate.
"Un-light, my dear, and go to bed;
You'll find your steed in the stables fed."

And when she entered her father's door,
Her aged father stood on the floor.

[1] This line and the concluding one in the stanza above were not sung by Mr. Hayes when the version was originally sent to Mrs. Flanders by mail on December 30, 1940. The 1940 text was used in *Ballads Migrant in New England*, 145.

Saying, "Father dear, did you send for me
By such a messenger, kind sir?" said she.

The hair rose on the old man's head
For he knew quite well her true love was dead.
He wrung his hands and wept full sore
But this young man's darling wept ten times more.

A short while after a little space,
They both arrived at this young man's grave.
Although his body was six weeks dead,
Her Holland handkerchief was 'round his head.

So come, all young maidens, a warning take.
Beware, and not your vows to break.
My vows are broke; my true love's gone.
I ne'er can call him back again.

C

*"The Suffolk Miracle" as sung by Franklin Smith, father of
Herbert Wilson Smith, a mining engineer in Washington,
D. C., whose relatives, Mr. and Mrs. F. E. Hartwell of
Bolton, Vermont, sing his father's tunes. The songs, which
the father wrote down from memory, had little inked crosses
for periods, in the old manner. He also wrote in parentheses
different ways in which he remembered the songs. Copied
literatim et punctatim.*

H. H. F., Collector
August 7, 1957

No Title

In old York town there once did dwell
A fair young lady straight and tall
The lads they came from near and far (far and wide)
They came to court her one and all.

They came with sighs and pretty words
But she had eyes for only one.
To win her favor and her love
He was the wealthy squires son.

When her father came to know her wish
He sent her far from home
Three hundred miles or more she went
With broken heart alone.

The young man sighed he mourned he wept
And very soon the young man died
And he had been a twelve month dead
When he drew by the fair maids side

"I've ridden far on this white steed
To be here at your side
I've brought to you your mother's cloak
And back with me you'll ride."

"Your father's steed your mother's cloak
Round my eyes your kerchief white
Take your postillion place with me
We'll ride all through the night"

They rode all night until the day
And came then to her father's door
"Now I will put this white steed away"
But him she never saw no more.

"You're welcome home her" father said
"How came you to be here?"
"You sent to me my own true love
The one I hold most dear."

Her father's hair rose on his head
To hear his daughter's words

The squire's son now twelve month dead
And laying in his shroud.

To young and old to great and small
The father then did say
"Let not your pride bring on your fall
In Love let young love have its way."

Our Goodman

(Child 274)

Mrs. Sullivan's statement that "Our Goodman" is a drinking song" into which is "put . . . anything they like" is an accurate description of this usually bawdy piece. It has been known in Britain at least since the end of the eighteenth century and a German translation of an English broadside started its spread across Europe during the early nineteenth century. Generally, the American texts are Scottish in form, like Child A, but as a rule they attempt to soften the cuckolding of the husband by making him a drunkard. Note, however, Flanders G.

See Coffin, 144–5 (American); Dean–Smith, 70 (English); and Greig and Keith, 214–6 (Scottish) for a start on a bibliography. Child, V, 88 f., discusses the use of the motif in literary and folk tales.

Many informants refuse to sing this ballad on moral grounds, though the lines that have caused them to feel this way are not to be found in print.

A

As given H. H. F. by Herbert Wilson Smith, mining engineer in Washington, D. C., as handwritten by his father, Franklin Smith. In parentheses are given different ways the song was remembered. Copied literatim et punctatim.

H. H. F., Collector
August 7, 1957

Last night when I came home
As drunk as I could be
I thought I saw another hat
Where my hat ought to be.

"O dear wife   O fond wife
O darling wife says I
Whose hat is that hat
(Where my hat ought to lie)   *alternate*
With the gautlet gloves near by?"

"O you big fool   you old fool
You're drunk as drunk can be
It's nothing but a stewing pot
My mother sent to me."

"O dear wife   O fond wife
I've travelled the wide world o'er
But a stew pot with a lining in
I never saw before"

*   *   *   *   *   *   *

Last night when I came home
As drunk as I could be
I thought I saw another coat
Where my coat ought to be

"O dear wife   O fond wife
O darling wife says I
Whose coat is that coat
With the stirrup boots near by"
(Where my coat ought to lie?")

"O you big fool   you old fool
You're drunk as drunk can be
It's nothing but a dinny bag
My father sent to me."

"O dear wife   O fond wife
I've travelled the wide world o'er
But a dinny bag with a collar on
I never saw before$_x$"

Last night when I came home
As drunk as I could be
I thought I saw another horse
Where my horse ought to be

"O dear wife   O fond wife
O darling wife says I
Whose horse is that horse
What made my horse to shy"

"You big fool   you old fool
You're drunk as drunk can be
It's only that old muley cow
My brother sent to me"

"O dear wife   O fond wife
I've travelled the wide world o'er
But a muley cow with a saddle on
I never saw before."

Last night when I came home
As drunk as drunk could be
I thought I saw another head
Laid where my head should be$_x$

"O dear wife   O fond wife
O darling wife says I
Whose head is that head
Where my head ought to lie"

You big fool   you old fool
You're drunk as drunk can be
It's nothing but dear sister's head
Who's come to visit me."

O dear wife   O fond wife
(I've travelled the wide world o'er)
Don't tell me any more
Your sister with a mustache on
I never saw before$_x$"

x

B

*Recited by Thomas C. Keyes, Newbury, Vermont, as sung
by a nurse who at that time was still living at an advanced
age in South Ryegate, Vermont.*

Phillips Barry, Collector
April, 1906

Our Good Man

The old man came home at night
As tired as he could be,
And found another man's hat
Where his hat ought to be.
"O wife, dearest wife,
How came this to be—
Another man's hat
Where mine ought to be?"

"Oh, you old fool, you blind fool,
Oh, can you never see?
That's nothing but a hood
Your mother sent to me!"
"Oh, miles have I traveled,
Hundreds and thousands more,
But never saw a hood
With stiff brim and crown before!"

The old man came home at night
As tired as he could be,

And found another man's coat
Where his coat ought to be.
"Oh, wife, dearest wife,
How came this to be,—
Another man's coat
Where mine ought to be?"

"Oh, you old fool, you blind fool,
Oh, can you never see?
That's nothing but a petticoat
Your mother sent to me!"
"Oh, miles have I traveled,
Hundreds and thousands more,
But never saw a petticoat
With sleeves (buttons) on before!"

In the same way, the old wife asserts that a strange
horse in the stable is

"Nothing but a milking cow."

C

As sung by Josiah S. Kennison of Searsburg, Vermont, who
learned this in an itinerant life as barker at fairs, scissors
grinder, clockmender, etc.

H. H. F. Collector
Early 1930's

The old man came home
His dear old wife to see.
He found a horse in his stall
Where his horse ought to be.

"O wife, dearest wife,
Will you explain to me
Whose horse is in my stall
Where my horse ought to be?"

"You old fool, you blind fool,
Drunk or can't you see?
'Tis nothing but a sawhorse
My mother sent to me."

The old man came home
His dear old wife to see;
He found a bonnet on a white-a-birch
Where his bonnet ought to be.

"O wife, dearest wife,
Will you explain to me
Whose hat's on my peg
Where my hat ought to be?"

"You old fool, you blind fool,
Blind, or can't you see?
'Tis nothing but a sunbonnet
My mother sent to me."

D

D. H. Raymond of Springfield, Vermont, sang this song as learned from his father Alexander Raymond (deceased).
H. H. F., Collector

Our Good Man

"Wife, dearest wife, come quick and tell to me
Whose coat this is, in the place my own coat ought to be."

"You darn fool, you crazy fool, you're blind and cannot see.
Isn't that the petticoat my granny sent to me?"

"I've travelled this world over; I've travelled miles and miles
But buttons on a petticoat I never saw before.

"Wife, dearest wife, come quick and tell to me
Whose head this is in the place where my own head ought
     to be."

"You darn fool, you crazy fool, you're drunk and cannot see.
Isn't that the cabbage head my mother sent to me?"

"I've travelled this world over; I've travelled door to door,
But hair upon a cabbage head I never saw before."

E

*Sung by Elwin Burditt of Springfield, Vermont, as learned
in Alpena, Michigan.*

H. H. F., Collector

Our Good Man

"For many miles I've travelled,
For many miles or more,
But I never saw a puddin' stick
With a gold head on before."

"You damn fool, you blind fool,
Why can't you ever see,
It's nothing but a cow
My mother sent to me?"

"Many miles I have travelled,
Ten thousand miles or more,
But stirrups on a cow
I never saw before."

F

*Fragment remembered by H. S. Sandelin of Springfield,
Vermont, as sung by his wife's stepfather, John Heath, formerly of northern Vermont, now of Waterville, Qubec.*

H. H. F., Collector

Our Good Man

Found a horse in the stable
Where his own horse ought to be.

"Wife dear, wife dear,
. . . .

. . . .

. . . .

"You old fool, you blind fool,
Can't you ever see
This is a cow
That my mother sent to me?"

. . . .

. . . .

And a saddle on a cow
I never saw before."

G

Mrs. Ellen M. Sullivan of Springfield, Vermont, called this a "drinking song." She said any one put into it anything they liked. When urged to sing it, she furnished this form.

H. H. F., *Collector*
August, 1932.

Our Good Man

"What brought that horse here, where it should not be?"
"Blind Sally Cockhold and blind you may be,
Don't you see that's a sow pig my mama sent to me?"
"Miles I have travelled, many miles or more,
But a saddle on a sow pig I never saw before!"

"What brought that hat there, where it should not be?"
"Blind Sally Cockhold and blind you may be,
Don't you see that that's a skimming dish my mama sent
     to me?'
"Miles I have travelled, many miles or more,
And such a hairy skimming dish I never saw before!"

"What brought that coat there, where it should not be?"
"Blind Sally Cockhold and blind you may be,
Don't you see that that's a blanket my mama sent to me?"
"Miles I have travelled, many miles or more,
And buttons on a blanket I never saw before!"

Get Up and Bar the Door

(Child 275)

Child stresses in his headnote to "Get Up and Bar the Door" that the domestic quarrel behind this song, or quarrels quite like it, have formed the basis of a host of folk and popular tales from Europe and Asia. (See Aarne–Thompson, Mt. 1351.) It has also been known, usually in a ribald form, among British and American college students for many generations. However, even though all this is true and even though it appeared in a number of nineteenth-century songsters, it is not much of a favorite with the American folk.

The usual American form of the ballad is the Scottish Child A, and the texts in Phillips Barry, *British Ballads from Maine*, 318; Greig and Keith, 216; and the Flanders Collection all parallel that version closely. See Coffin, 145–6, for a start on an American bibliography. It has been printed in many musical anthologies. Of particular interest along this line is the burlesque in Delehanty and Hengler's *Song and Dance Book* of 1874.

As sung by Mrs. Frances Kilbride of Brookline, Massachusetts, who learned it from hearing her father, Frank Mac-Gregor, sing it. Mr. MacGregor was born in Scotland, and came to this country with his daughter, Mrs. Kilbride, who was twenty-four years of age at the time. Mrs. Kilbride was born in Glasgow. When three months old she was taken by her parents to the North Coast (outside of Aberdeen), at which place she remained until coming to America. Mrs. Kilbride says, "This used to be one of my father's favorite songs."

M. Olney, Collector
September 21, 1953

Structure: A B C D (4,4,4,3); Rhythm B; Contour: undulating; Scale: pentachordal

t.c. B flat. Note the repeated tone at the beginning.

For mel. rel. see FCB4, 112; MF, 320; BES, 318; GCM, 371 (all very close)

The Barrin' o' Oor Door

Tr.M.O.

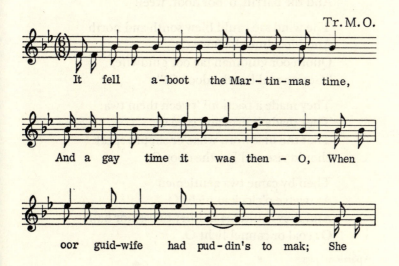

boiled   them   in   the   pan - O; And   the

bar - rin'   o'   oor   door,   weel,___ weel, ___

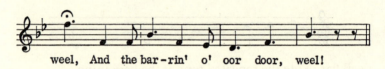

weel, And   the bar-rin'   o'   oor   door,   weel!

The Barrin' o' Oor Door

It fell aboot the Martinmas time
And a gay time it was then-O,
When oor guidwife had puddin's to mak;
She boiled then in the pan-O;
And the barrin' o' oor door, weel, weel, weel,
And the barrin' o' oor door, weel!

The wind sae cauld blew south and north
And blew into the floor-O;
Quoth oor guidman tae oor guidwife,
"Get up and bar the door-O!"

They made a paction[1] 'tween them twa;
They made it firm and sure-O,
That the first word whae'er should speak
Should rise and bar the door-O.

Then by came twa gentlemen
At twelve o'clock at nicht-O
And they could see neither hoose nor hall
Or coal or cannel-licht-O.

[1] paction: pact.

"Now what if this be a rich man's hoose,
Or what if it be a pair-O?" [2]
But ne'er a word wad ane of them speak
For barrin' o' the door-O.

And first they ate the white puddin's
And then they ate the black-O,
Though muckle thocht the guidwife to herself
Yet ne'er ane word she spoke-O.

Then said the ane untae the ither,
"Here, man, tak ye my knife-O,
Dae ye tak off the auld man's beard
And I'll kiss the guidwife-O.

"But there's nae water in the hoose
And what will we do then-O?"
"What ails ye at the puddin-brew
That boils in the pan-O?"

O up then got oor guidman
And an angry man was he-O.
"Will ye kiss me wife afore my een
And sca'd me wi' puddin'-brew-O?"

Then up started oor guidwife,
Gi'ed three skips on the floor-O.
"Guidman, you've spoken the foremost word,
So get up and bar the door-O."

[2] pair: poor.

The Wife Wrapped in Wether's Skin
(Child 277)

This ballad derives from an old tale which Child, V, 104, cites under the title "The Wife Lapped in Morrel's Skin" and is related to a whole host of stories on similar themes. See Aarne–Thompson, Mt. 1370*.

The ballad is still popular in America, where the basic outline of the story remains constant, but where the minor details vary greatly. William H. Jansen has made a careful study (*HFQ*, IV, #3, 41) of the ballad and its developments in America, and from his remarks two groupings of the American texts emerge: songs with the "dandee, clish ma clinge" refrains, popular in the South and Midwest; and songs with the "juniper, gentian, and rosemary" refrains, popular in the South and Northeast. The plant refrains of the latter group have caused some comment. Phillips Barry, *British Ballads from Maine*, 324–5, suggests, on the authority of Lucy Broadwood (*JFSS*, II, 12–15), that the wife originally was beaten to exorcise the evil spirits that infested her and that "juniper, gentian, and rosemary" were regarded as charms against the demons. Later the names of the plants were forgotten and confused with the names of girls, June, Jenny, and Rose Mary.

The Flanders texts are highly representative of the American forms of the ballad. A–I, with the plant refrain, relate to Child F (from Massachusetts) and are normal Northeastern versions. J–L illustrate the "dandee" refrain and the common "old man who lived in the West" opening.

M–N (see also Child C) are from Scottish tradition. Text L, which concerns "Riddleson's daughter Dinah," is the only unusual version in the group.

See Coffin, 146–8 (American); Belden, 92–94 (English); and Greig and Keith, 218–20 (Scottish) for bibliographical material and discussion.

All of the tunes for Child 277 except the Richards tune are members of the same tune family. Within this group, the Prevost and Baldwin tunes are especially close, as are the Hayward and Hall tunes. The Monson tune is slightly outside the group.

A

Sung by Mrs. Lena Bourne Fish of East Jaffrey, New Hampshire, as learned from her father, Stratton Bourne, who was born in northern Vermont. Mr. Bourne's forebears were the early settlers of Bourne, Massachusetts, on Cape Cod.[1]

M. Olney, Collector
March 6, 1942

Me Old Wether's Skin

I married a wife in the month of June,
Dainty fair Jennie Rose Marie;
I think I married a little too soon,
As the dew flies over the mulberry tree.
I think I married a little too soon,
As the dew flies over the green valley.

Me wife would not cook; she would not card or spin,
Dainty fair Jennie Rose Marie,
For fear she would soil her lily-white skin,
As the dew flies over the mulberry tree;
For fear she would soil her lily-white skin,
As the dew flies over the green valley.

[1] Mrs. Fish sang the song again on August 26, 1943, in an identical version.

One day I came in from jogging the plow,
   Dainty fair Jennie Rose Marie,
Saying, "Good wife, is me dinner done now?"
   As the dew flies over the mulberry tree;
Saying, "Good wife, is me dinner done now?"
   As the dew flies over the green valley.

"There's bread and there's cheese upon the shelf,"
   Said dainty fair Jennie Rose Marie;
"If you want any dinner, go get it yourself,"
   As the dew flies over the mulberry tree.
"If you want any dinner, go get it yourself,"
   As the dew flies over the green valley.

Then out to the sheep-pen I ran with haste,
   Dainty fair Jennie Rose Marie,
And I killed the bell-wether without any waste,
   As the dew flies over the mulberry tree;
I killed the bell-wether without any waste,
   As the dew flies over the green valley.

I took out me knife and went snippety snip,
   Dainty fair Jennie Rose Marie,
And I pulled off his hide by the strippety strip,
   As the dew flies over the mulberry tree;
I pulled off his hide by the strippety strip,
   As the dew flies over the green valley.

I then threw the sheepskin across me wife's back,
   Dainty fair Jennie Rose Marie,
And with two sticks I went whickety whack,
   As the dew flies over the mulberry tree;
And with two sticks I went whickety whack,
   As the dew flies over the green valley.

"I'll tell me brothers and all of my kin,"
   Said dainty fair Jennie Rose Marie,

"For to beat your wife is surely a sin,"
  As the dew flies over the mulberry tree;
"To beat your wife is surely a sin,"
  As the dew flies over the green valley.

"You may tell your brothers and all your kin,"
  Dainty fair Jennie Rose Marie,
"But I'm bound to tan me old wether's skin,"
  As the dew flies over the mulberry tree;
"I'm bound to tan me old wether's skin,"
  As the dew flies over the green valley.

She now cooks me dinner and sets up the board,
  Dainty fair Jennie Rose Marie,
With a smile of contentment at every word,
  As the dew flies over the mulberry tree;
With a smile of contentment at every word,
  As the dew flies over the green valley.

She is a fine cook; she can both card and spin,
  Dainty fair Jennie Rose Marie,
Since the day I tanned me old wether's skin,
  As the dew flies over the mulberry tree;
Since the day I tanned me old wether's skin,
  As the dew flies over the green valley.

B

Charles Wade of Wallingford, Vermont, has known this
song most of his seventy-seven years.

H. H. F., Collector
October 3, 1934

Wife Wrapped in Wether's Skin

I married me a wife by the light of the moon,
  Tella flow gentle Rosa Marie,
Though fear that I had married too soon,
  As the dew flies over the mulberry tree.

As I came in from jogging my plow,
Tella flow gentle Rosa Marie,
Saying, "Dear wife, have you dinner for me now?"
As the dew flies over the mulberry tree.

She call-ed me a sassy old whelp,
Tella flow gentle Rosa Marie;
"If you want any dinner, you can get it yourself."
As the dew flies over the mulberry tree.

I took my knife, went out to the yard,
Tella flow gentle Rosa Marie;
I ketched a wether as it passed my bard,
As the dew flies over the mulberry tree.

I cut his throat, took off his skin,
Tella flow gentle Rosa Marie;
I cut him in quarters and I carried him in,
As the dew flies over the mulberry tree.

I stretched the skin on my wife's back,
Tella flow gentle Rosa Marie,
And every blow went whickety whack,
As the dew flies over the mulberry tree.

"O husband dear, don't beat me so,
Tella flow gentle Rosa Marie;
I'll be your boy and drive your plow."
As the dew flies over the mulberry tree.

"I care for you or any your help,
Tella flow gentle Rosa Marie;
I'll get a boy or drive it myself."
As the dew flies over the mulberry tree.

"I have brothers, one, two by three,
Tella flow gentle Rosa Marie,
If they were here, you wouldn't beat me."
As the dew flies over the mulberry tree.

"I care for you or any your kin,
Tella flow gentle Rosa Marie,
But your old back shall tan my skin."
As the dew flies over the mulberry tree.

C

As sung by George Edwards of Burlington, Vermont.

H. H. F., *Collector*

Structure: A Bᵃ C Dᶜ C Dᶜ (2,2,2,2,2,2); Rhythm B; Contour: descending; Scale: Aeolian

t.c. A.

For mel. rel. see Sharp 1, 272 C; 273 D; BES, 323.

As the Dew Flies over the Green Vallee

Tr. M. O.

And now he brings a gen-tle wife;
Jun-i-per gen-tle Rose-Ma-rie; And
though she's not par-tic-ul-'ly bright, As the
dew flies o-ver the green val-lee.

As the Dew Flies Over the Green Vallee

And now he brings a gentle wife;
>Juniper gentle Rose-Marie;
And though she's not particul'ly bright,
>As the dew flies over the green vallee.
And though she's not particul'ly bright,
>As the dew flies over the green vallee.

But she can't card nor she can't spin
For fear of spoiling her delicate skin.

Now he comes in, comes in from plough,
And says, "Dear wife, is your dinner done now?"

She call-ed him a saucy whelp;
"If you want any dinner—go get it yourself!"

And out he goes to the sheep-fold
And drawers the big fat wether to the pole.

He wraps the skin on his wife's back
And with two sticks he went whickety-whack.

"I'll tell my parents and my kin!
To beat my back is surely a sin!"

"You may tell your parents and your kin!
I'm beating nothing but my wether's skin."

And now she spins and spins and cards
And says, "Dear one, your dinner is done."

She hauls the table, spreads the board,
And "O dear husband," with every word.

And ever since that, she's been a good wife;
I hope she remains so all the days of her life.

D

Recorded from the singing of Louis Prevost, in Springfield, Vermont, as learned from his mother, Alma Foster Prevost (born 1848). Published in Vermont Folk-Songs & Ballads, *224, and in* A Garland of Green Mountain Song, *84.*

George Brown, Collector
December, 1931

Structure: A B C D (4,4,4,4); Rhythm D; Contour: generally ascending; Scale: pentatonic with half-tone

t.c. C.

For mel. rel. see FCB4, 114 D.

The Wife Wrapped in Wether's Skin

The Wife Wrapped in Wether's Skin

Billy married a wife and he carried her home.
Jenny go gently, Rose Marie,
Think he'd better had let her alone,
As the dew flies over the mulberry tree.

(Follow pattern for next verses.)

She would not into the kitchen go,
Afraid of soiling her kid white shoes.

She would not card, she would not spin,
Afraid of soiling her lily-white skin.

One day when Billy came home from the plough,
Saying, "My dear wife, is dinner ready now?"

"Go off, go off, you ugly elf;
If you want any dinner you'll get it yourself."

Down to the sheepfold Billy did go,
Out with a wether without control;

Out with his knife went rip, rip, rip,
And off went the pelt, strip, strip, strip.

He threw the hide upon her back
And with two sticks went whickety whack.

"I have brothers, one, two, three.
If they knew this, you wouldn't lick me."

"What care I for kith or kin;
I've a right to tan my own sheepskin."

She up to the table, on with the board;
'Twas "Yes, sir," "No, sir," every word.

She proved to Billy a kind good wife.
He loved her as he loved his life.

E

*As sung by Mrs. George Hayward of Springfield, Vermont.
Learned from her grandmother, Mrs. Kathryn Cushman,
of Scottish descent.*

H. H. F., Collector
May, 1932

Structure: A B C D (2,2,2,2); Rhythm D; Contour: undulating; Scale: major

t.c. G.

The Wife Wrapped in Wether's Skin

Tr. M. O.

Bil-ly got a wife and he brought her home,

Jen-nie throw-a-gen - tle - a   ro - sa-ma-ree.   He

might had done— bet-ter if he'd left— her a-lone,

As the dew flies o - ver the   mul-ber-ry tree.

The Wife Wrapped in Wether's Skin

Billy got a wife and he brought her home,
    Jennie throw-a-gentle-a, ro-sama-ree.
He might had done better if he'd left her alone,
    As the dew flies over the mulberry tree.

She would not into the kitchie go,
For 'fraid of soiling her white kid shoes.

She would not carve or she would not spin,
'Fraid of soiling her gay gold ring.

Billy went down to the old sheep's fold,
Cut him a stick of willow so green.

"I have brothers, one, two, three;
If they were here, you wouldn't whip me!"

"What care I for your nine or ten brothers?
I'm able to tan my own sheepskin!"

She out with a tablecloth and spread it on the board.
Never a word yet said: "Yes" or "No."

F

*Luther Weeks of Springfield, Vermont, recalled the follow-
ing lines. The words fit the tune given in version G by his
sister, Mrs. Wallace Baldwin.*

H. H. F., Collector
Late 1932

She would not card and she would not spin,
Jinny fare jintle, Rose-a-Marie,
For fear of spoiling her gay gold ring,
As the dew flies over the green vallee.

She would not into the kitchen go,
Jinny fare jintle, Rose-a-Marie,
For fear of spoiling her high-heeled shoe,
As the dew flies over the green vallee.

(*When he kills a wether and puts its skin over her back
before beating it—and her—she sings:*)

"I'll tell my parents and my kin,
Jinny fare jintle, Rose-a-Marie,
That you've whipped my back till I'm sore within,"
As the dew flies over the green vallee.

"You may tell your parents and your kin,
Jinny fare jintle, Rose-a-Marie,

That I've whipped your back till you're sore within,
But I've whipped nothing but my old sheep skin."
As the dew flies over the green vallee.

G

Recorded from the singing of Mrs. Wallace Baldwin of Springfield, Vermont, who learned this during her childhood spent at Twenty Mile Stream, near Cavendish, Vermont.

H. H. F., Collector
May, 1932

Structure: A B A C (2,2,2,2); Rhythm C; Contour: undulating; Scale: hexatonic

t.c. F. Note the small range (major sixth).

For mel. rel. see FCB4, 114 D.

Wife Wrapped in Wether's Skin

Tr. M. O.

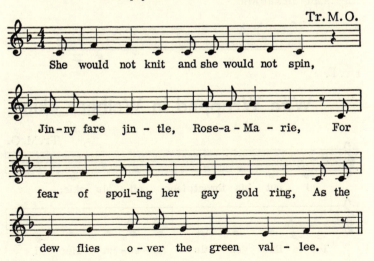

She would not knit and she would not spin,

Jin-ny fare jin - tle, Rose-a - Ma - rie, For

fear of spoil-ing her gay gold ring, As the

dew flies o - ver the green val - lee.

Wife Wrapped in Wether's Skin

She would not knit and she would not spin,
    Jinny fare jintle, Rose-a-Marie,
For fear of spoiling her gay gold ring,
    As the dew flies over the green vallee.

She would not into the kitchen go,
    Jinny fare jintle, Rose-a-Marie,
For fear of spoiling her high-heeled shoes,
    As the dew flies over the green vallee.

. . . .
. . . .

He took her by the heels and went a-dragging her along,
    As the dew flies over the green vallee.

H

As sung by E. F. Hall of Ludlow, Vermont.

                        H. H. F., Collector

Structure: A B C D (2,2,2,2); Rhythm C; Contour: undulating; Scale: hexatonic

t. c. F.

Wife Wrapped in Wether's Skin

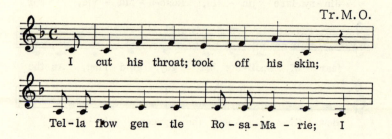

cut   him in quar-ters and I   car-ried him   in,

As the dew flies   o - ver the mul - ber-ry tree.

Wife Wrapped in Wether's Skin

I cut his throat; took off his skin;
  Tella flow gentle Rosa-Marie,
I cut him in quarters and I carried him in;
  As the dew flies over the mulberry tree.

I stretched the skin on my wife's back;
And every blow went whickety-whack.

"O husband dear, don't beat me so,
I'll be your boy and drive your plough!

"I have brothers, one, two by three;
If they were here, you wouldn't beat me!"

"I care not for. . . .

I

As sung by Mrs. Mabel Pease of Orford, New Hampshire.
M. Olney, Collector
November 19, 1942

Structure: A B C D D (2,2,2,2,2); Rhythm mostly A; Contour: arc; Scale: major

t.c. D.

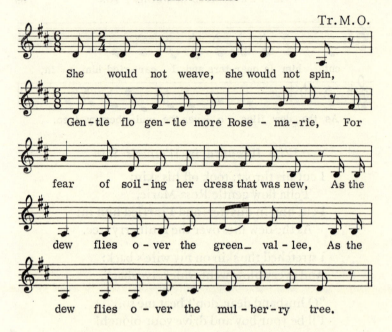

She would not weave, she would not spin,
Gentle flo gentle more Rose-marie,
For fear of soiling her dress that was new,
As the dew flies over the green vallee,
As the dew flies over the mulberry tree.

J

*Furnished by Edward Richards of Warren, Connecticut, as
he remembered the singing of his mother, a native of those
parts. Published in* Ballads Migrant in New England, *221.*

H. H. F., *Collector*
August 31, 1949

Structure: A B C D E F (2,2,2,2,1,3); Rhythm A; Contour:
undulating; Scale: hexatonic

t.c. G.

For mel. rel. see Sharp 1, 271 A; DV, 597 No. 45 (D).

Wife Wrapped in Wether's Skin

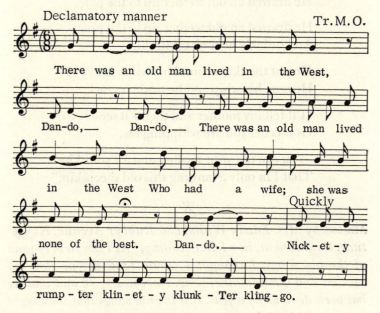

Declamatory manner   Tr. M. O.

There was an old man lived in the West,

Dan-do,— Dan-do,— There was an old man lived

in the West Who had a wife; she was

none of the best. Dan-do.— Nick-et-y

rump-ter klin-et-y klunk-Ter kling-go.

Wife Wrapped in Wether's Skin

There was an old man lived in the West,
    Dan-do, Dan-do,
There was an old man lived in the West
Who had a wife; she was none of the best.
    Dan-do.
Nickety rumpter klinety klunk—
Ter kling-go.

(Follow pattern for next stanzas.)

One morning the old man came in from plow,
Saying, "Wife, is breakfast ready now?"

"There's a crust of bread lies on the shelf;
If you want anything, go help yourself."

The old man went out to his sheepfold;
He drawed an old wether up to the pole.

He drawed an old wether up to the pin,
And quickly he took off its skin.

He put the skin around his wife's back;
He took his whip and he made it crack.

"I'll tell my mother and then I'll see
How cruel you are whipping me."

"You can tell your mother and all your kin
That I'm only a-tanning this old sheepskin."

K

Mailed by Mrs. Edwin White, 686 Rubber Avenue, Nauga-
tuck, Connecticut, in a letter reading, "As I am so very fond
of the old songs, I thought I would send in one that my
Mother and Grandmother sang. I am nearly 70 and mother
has been dead many a year. But the old songs that she taught
me are still fresh in my memory." Copied literatim et punc-
tatim.

H. H. F., *Collector*
March 28, 1949

There was an old man lived in the West.
He had an old wife she was none of the best.

One day the old man came in from plow
Saying Wife is breakfast ready now.

There is a crust lies on the shelf.
If you want anything just help your self.

The old man went out to his sheep fold.
He drew an old sheep up to the pole.

He drew an old sheep up to the pin.
And rapidly took off her skin

He put the skin around his wife's back
he took his whip and made it crack.

"I'll tell my mother and all I see
How crully you are treating me.

You may tell your mother and all your kin.
I was only tanning my old sheepskin

L

Sent by mail by Beulah Dix Flebbe of 636 Las Casas Avenue, Pacific Palisades, California, who writes of this song: "This was sung to me by my mother. I was born in 1876, so you see, that was quite a while ago. My mother, Maria Dix, was born in Machias, Maine, in 1848. Her parents were Samuel Morse (whose father came from York state about 1800) and Christiana Milliken. Christiana's parents were John Milliken and Sarah Brown, of St. Stephen's, New Brunswick. I've always had a notion that this came down from Sarah Brown, who was, as her name might imply, of Scots descent." Copied literatim et punctatim.

H. H. F., *Collector*
March 20, 1946

Structure: A B C D (2,2,2,2) ; Rhythm D; Contour: descending; Scale: tetratonic

t.c. F.

Riddleson's Daughter, Dinah

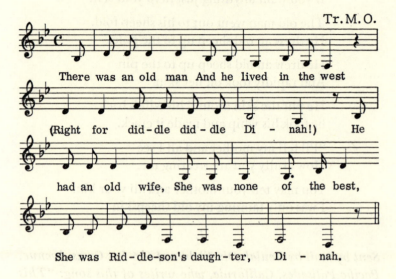

Tr. M. O.

There was an old man And he lived in the west

(Right for did-dle did-dle Di - nah!) He

had an old wife, She was none of the best,

She was Rid-dle-son's daugh-ter, Di - nah.

Riddleson's Daughter, Dinah

THERE was an old man
And he lived in the west—
(Right for diddle diddle Dinah!)
He had an old wife,
She was none of the best,
She was Riddleson's daughter, Dinah.

Oh, I won't bake,
And I won't brew,
(Right for diddle diddle Dinah!)
And I won't make
My white hands black,
For I'm Riddleson's daughter, Dinah.

The old man went out
And he got a stick,
(Right for diddle diddle Dinah!)

And whickety whack
Went over her back,
Though she's Riddleson's daughter, Dinah.

Oh, I will bake
And I will brew,
(Right for diddle diddle Dinah!)
And I will work out
In the kit-*chin*,
Though I'm Riddleson's daughter, Dinah.

And then, good husband,
If that won't do,
(Right for diddle diddle Dinah!)
I'll stoop down and
Buckle up your shoe,
Though I'm Riddleson's daughter, Dinah.

M

Recorded by George Brown from the singing of Miss Stella E. Monson of North Wardsboro, Vermont. Learned in New Haven, Connecticut, by Miss Monson in 1885 from the singing of the Patterson family, who had just come over from Aberdeen, Scotland. Printed in Vermont Folk-Songs & Ballads, *222.*

George Brown, Collector
August 23, 1930

Structure: A B C D E (2,2,2,2,2) ; Rhythm A; Contour: arc; Scale: major

t.c. G.

For mel. rel. see BP, 41 (not too close).

Cooper of Fife

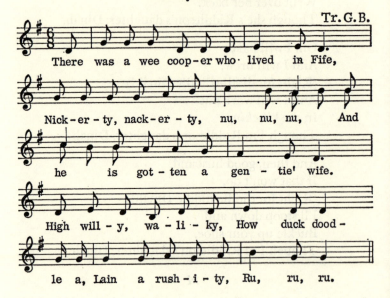

Tr. G. B.

There was a wee coop-er who lived in Fife,
Nick-er-ty, nack-er-ty, nu, nu, nu, And
he is got-ten a gen-tie' wife.
High will-y, wa-li-ky, How duck dood-
le a, Lain a rush-i-ty, Ru, ru, ru.

Cooper of Fife

There was a wee cooper who lived in Fife,
Nickerty, nackerty, nu, nu, nu,
And he is gotten a gentie' wife.
> High willy, waliky,
> How duck doodle a,
> Lain a rushity,
> Ru, ru, ru.

She wadna' bake an' she wadna' brew,
Nickerty, nackerty, nu, nu, nu,
For fear of spoiling her comely hue.
> High willy, waliky,
> How duck doodle a,
> Lain a rushity,
> Ru, ru, ru.

And she wadna' wash and she wadna' wring,
Nickerty, nackerty, nu, nu, nu,
For the fear of spoiling her braw gold ring.
>High willy, waliky,
>How duck doodle a,
>Lain a rushity,
>Ru, ru, ru.

She wadna' card and she wadna' spin,
Nickerty, nackerty, nu, nu, nu,
With the fear of offending her high-bred kin.
>High willy, waliky,
>How duck doodle a,
>Lain a rushity,
>Ru, ru, ru.

The cooper has gone to his wool pack,
Nickerty, nackerty, nu, nu, nu,
An' has laid a sheepskin on his ain wife's back,
>High willy, waliky,
>How duck doodle a,
>Lain a rushity,
>Ru, ru, ru.

"I didna' thrash thee for your proud kin,
Nickerty, nackerty, nu, nu, nu,
But I'm sure I may thrash me own sheepskin."
>High willy, waliky,
>How duck doodle a,
>Lain a rushity,
>Ru, ru, ru.

Now all you have gotten a gentie' wife,
Nickerty, nackerty, nu, nu, nu,
Take example by the cooper of Fife,
>High willy, waliky,
>How duck doodle a,

Lain a rushity,
Ru, ru, ru.

N

Sent by Miss Margaret Houston of Westerly, Rhode Island.
H. H. F., Collector
March, 1945

The Wife Wrapped in Wether's Skin

There was a wee cooper. He lived
in Fife.
Hey Willy Walliky, Hi John Toogle.
Took unto himself a gentle wife.
Hey Willy Walliky, Hi John Toogle,
Toodle, oodle, loo.

She couldna' cook and she couldna'
shoo (sew)
Hey Willy Walliky, Hi John Toogle.

The Farmer's Curst Wife

(Child 278)

There is an old proverb that says there are but two places where a man wants to have his wife—in bed and in the grave. Certainly, the scolding wife, one who can rout the devil himself, has left her mark on folklore from India and Russia to the Western countries. This particular anecdote concerning her is a favorite of the American informant. With a similar song, "The Devil in Search of a Wife," it was also popular among the printers of nineteenth-century London broadsides.

Originally, it must have concerned a contract in which a farmer hired the devil to do some plowing in exchange for a member of the family. The farmer, in many texts, worries that he may lose his eldest son and is relieved when his wife is taken. The American versions follow Child A as a rule, it being rare that the wife come back to her cooking as in Child B. However, the yoking of the dogs and hogs to the plow and the proverbial sayings at the close of the song are frequently added to the Child A base in the New World.

The Flanders material needs little comment. Texts A and B, in which the farmer seems to be rather proud of his wife's triumph over the forces of hell are not common, though Phillips Barry, *British Ballads from Maine,* 330–1, prints an example from Northeast Harbor. Nor are the C–I "Anthony Rowley" texts with the "right leg, left leg" refrains. But C, in which the wife is the farmer, harnesses the cattle herself, and goes to the gates of hell, is the only text that introduces a really radical story variation. C is a noteworthy find.

American references for Child 278 may be found in Coffin, 148–50. See also Dean–Smith, 66, and Belden, 94–95, for English citations. Barry, *op. cit.*, 332, cites local uses of the motif in New England.

The tunes for Child 278 all belong to one tune family. A large proportion of them are especially closely related; the following tunes are slightly divergent: Ordway, Davis, Weeks, Brackett. The Underhill, Farnham, and Lorette tunes are very similar, as are the Moses and Blake tunes.

For general relationship to the larger group of tunes, see FCB4, 116, 117, 119; DV, 598 No. 46 (C), 599 No. 46 (E) and (F), 601 No. 46 (L); GCM, 373; Sharp 1, 275, 278.

A

Recorded in Manchester Center, Vermont, from the singing of Paul Lorette, who learned this song from his brother, James Lorette, who learned it in the lumber woods near Ottawa, Canada.

George Brown, Collector
September 23, 1930

Structure: A B C D E (2,2,2,3,3); Rhythm A; Contour: undulating; Scale: hexatonic

t.c. C.

The Old Scolding Wife

There was an old man and he had a small farm,
     Fi-lee, fi-liddy, fi-low.

The Old Scolding Wife

Tr. M. O.

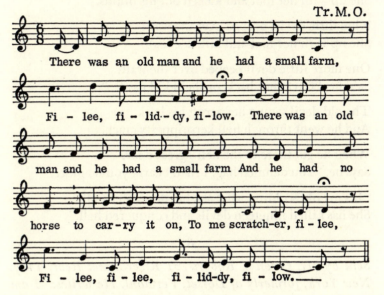

There was an old man and he had a small farm,
Fi - lee, fi - lid- - dy, fi - low. There was an old
man and he had a small farm And he had no
horse to car - ry it on, To me scratch-er, fi - lee,
Fi - lee, fi - lee, fi - lid-dy, fi - low.

There was an old man and he had a small farm
And he had no horse to carry it on,
    To me scratcher, fi-lee,
    Fi-lee, fi-lee, fi-liddy, fi-low.

(Follow same pattern for all stanzas.)

So he harnessed the pig and he bridled the sow,
And away he went, the devil knows how.

The old devil he came across the lot.
"It ain't you that I want; it's your old scolding wife.

"It ain't you that I want; it's your old scolding wife."
"Oh, take her, oh, take her out of my way."

The old devil he swung her acrost his back
And he went to hell kersnipperty crack.

She heard the old devil preparing his change;
She up with her foot and kicked out his brains.

Nine little devils peeped over the wall;
She up with her foot and killed 'em all.

One more little devil peeped over the wall;
Said he, "Carry her back, or she'll kill us all."

The old devil swung her acrost his back
And he went through hell kersnipperty crack.

When he got there to the hell's great door,
Says he, "You damned hag, I shan't carry you no more."

"It's my old scolding wife; she has done very well;
She has killed nineteen devils and conquered hell."

B

Sent by Mr. Owen S. Roberts, 31 River Street Rear, Troy, New York, formerly of Dorset, Vermont. He writes: "I am sending you my Great-grandmother's favorite song, 'Fie-Lillie, Fie-Lillie, Fie Lee, Fie-down.' I never heard anyone but my Great-grandmother sing this song; therefore it must be very old, and perhaps this is the only copy of it in existence. I do hope that you will find it suitable for your collection, that it may be preserved for future generations in remembrance of her, Lilla Jackson Wade, born and buried in Mount Holly, Vermont."

H. H. F., *Collector*
March 17, 1947

Fie-Lillie, Fie-Lillie, Fie-Lee, Fie-Down

There was an old farmer
Who owned a small farm,
Fie-lillie, fie-lillie, fie-lee, fie-down.
He had no horses to carry it on,

From a-scratch-a-fie-lee,
Fie-lillie, fie-lillie, fie-lee, fie-down.

So he hitched up his hogs
And away he did plow.
Fie-lillie, fie-lillie, fie-lee, fie-down.
This way, and that way,
The devil knows how,
From a-scratch-a-fie-lee,
Fie-lillie, fie-lillie, fie-lee, fie-down.

One day he saw the old devil a-coming,
Fie-lillie, fie-lillie, fie-lee, fie-down.
He thought he was after his oldest son,
From a-scratch-a-fie-lee,
Fie-lillie, fie-lillie, fie-lee, fie-down.

"Oh, it's not your oldest son,
But your old scolding wife,"
Fie-lillie, fie-lillie, fie-lee, fie-down.
"O take her, O take her, and hoping to God that you never
    will part,"
From a-scratch-a-fie-lee,
Fie-lillie, fie-lillie, fie-lee, fie-down.

Oh, the old devil, he slung her across his back,
Fie-lillie, fie-lillie, fie-lee, fie-down,
And down through hell he went, snappity-crack,
From a-scratch-a-fie-lee,
Fie-lillie, fie-lillie, fie-lee, fie-down.

Oh, when he got to hell's great door,
Fie-lillie, fie-lillie, fie-lee, fie-down.
He said, "Lay there, you old fool, I'll carry you no more,"
From a-scratch-a-fie-lee,
Fie-lillie, fie-lillie, fie-lee, fie-down.

Oh, she heard the old devil preparing his chains,
Fie-lillie, fie-lillie, fie-lee, fie-down.
She up with her foot and kicked out half of his brains,
From a-scratch-a-fie-lee,
Fie-lillie, fie-lillie, fie-lee, fie down.

One little devil said, "Hitch her up higher,"
Fie-lillie, fie-lillie, fie-lee, fie-down.
She up with her foot and kicked nine into the fire,
From a-scratch-fie-lee,
Fie-lillie, fie-lillie, fie-lee, fie-down.

One little devil peeked over the wall,
Fie-lillie-fie-lillie, fie-lee, fie-down.
Said, "Carry her back, or she'll kill us all,"
From a-scratch-a-fie-lee,
Fie-lillie, fie-lillie, fie-lee, fie-down.

The old devil, he slung her across his back,
Fie-lillie, fie-lillie, fie-lee, fie-down.
And like a broad-peddler, went tuggin' her back,
From a-scratch-a-fie-lee,
Fie-lillie, fie-lillie, fie-lee, fie-down.

"Oh, my old wife, she's done very well,
Fie-lillie, fie-lillie, fie-lee, fie-down.
She's killed all the devils, and conquered all hell,
From a-scratch-a-fie-lee,
Fie-lillie, fie-lillie, fie-lee, fie-down."

C

*Collected from Elwin Burditt of Springfield, Vermont,
heard in Shrewsbury, Vermont, sung by a boy of Irish
descent*

H. H. F., *Collector*
1931

The Scolding Wife

There was an old woman who hired a farm,
Come riddle, come riddle, come rally.
There was an old woman who hired a small farm
And she had no oxen to carry it on.
With a right leg, left leg, upper leg, under leg,
      over mo-rally.

(Follow pattern of first stanza for all stanzas.)

So she bridled her pig and she saddled her sow;
Then said the old woman, "I have them now."

And she drove cross-lots till she came to hell's gate
And she up with her leg and she kicked them straight.

Then said the old devil, "Let's put her up higher."
She up with her right leg and kicked nine in the fire.

Then said the old devil, "Let's put her down lower."
She up with her left leg and kicked nine more.

There was a little devil peeking over hell's wall,
And he said, "Put her out or she'll kill us all."

Then said the old woman, "Wasn't I brave?
I've been to hell and I've come back safe."

D

*As sung by Elmer George of North Montpelier, Vermont.
Mr. George says: "I don't recall where I learned it—it was
just popular and a lot of people used to sing it." When asked
if he had heard it sung in the woods he replied: "Oh, land
yes!"*

M. Olney, Collector
November 19, 1948

The Farmer's Curst Wife

There was an old man and he had him a farm.
Over Brave-Brown, come rowley.
There was an old man and he had him a farm
And he had no oxen to carry it on.
With his right leg, left leg, upper leg, under leg,
Over Brave-Brown, come rowley.

(*Follow pattern of first stanza for all stanzas.*)

He hitched up a dog along with a sow.
He yoked up the dog along with the sow.
And he fed him corn—the devil knows how.

"Oh!" says the old farmer, "it's now I'm undone,
For the devil's come after my only son!"

"Oh," says the old devil, "oh, don't go astray.
It's your damn scolding wife I'm to take away!"

"Oh, take her, oh, take her, with all my heart
And I hope to God that you never will part!"

Oh, the devil, he loaded her into his sack
And like a tin pedlar went clickty-clack.

He carried her down to hell's backdoor;
He give her a flop right on to the floor.

She saw the little devils a-rattling their chains,
She up with her foot and let out their brains.

Oh, one little devil peeks over the wall,
Saying, "Take her back—she'll kill us all!"
                       (. . . *spoken*)

Oh, the devil, he loaded her on to his back.
Oh, the old devil, he loaded her into his sack
And like a damn fool he went tugging her back.

"Oh, here is your wife and she is well,
She's licked the devil and conquered all hell!"

Now you see that the woman are worse than the men;
They can go to hell and back again!

E

*Asa Davis of Milton, Vermont, learned this from his father,
Joel Davis, of Duxbury, Vermont.*

H. H. F., *Collector*
June 23, 1939

Structure: A B¹ B² C D E (2,2,2,2,2,2); Rhythm A; Contour:
undulating; Scale: major

t.c. D.

The Farmer's Curst Wife

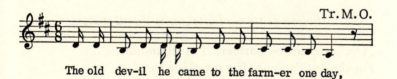

The old dev-il he came to the farm-er one day,

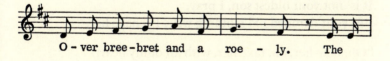

O - ver bree-bret and a   roe - ly.   The

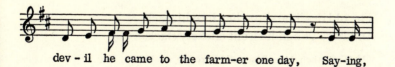

dev - il he came to the farm-er one day,   Say-ing,

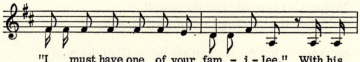

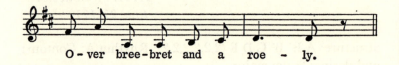

The Farmer's Curst Wife

The old devil he came to the farmer one day,
Over bree-bret and a roe-ly,
The devil he came to the farmer one day,
Saying, "I must have one of your familee."
With his right leg, left leg, upper leg, under leg,
Over bree-bret and a roe-ly.

(Follow pattern of first stanza for all stanzas.)

"Oh," cries the old farmer, "I'm all undone,
For the devil's come after my oldest son."

It is[1] not your oldest son, I pray,
But your damned old scolding wife. I'll have her."

"Oh, take her, oh, take her, with all of my heart,
And I hope to God you'll never part."

The old devil he slung her into his sack
And back to hell he went clickety clack.

[1] "'Tis" when Miss Olney did a retake on May 8, 1943.

The devils began to rattle their chains;[2]
She up with her foot and she kicked out their brains.

There was a young devil had on a blue cap;
She up with her foot and she ended that.

There was a little devil peeped over the wall,
Saying, "Carry her back, Daddy, she'll kill us all."

The old devil he slung her into his sack
And like an old fool he went tugging her back.

You see that the women are worse than the men,
For they'll git into hell and they git out again.

F

As sung by Luther Weeks of Springfield, Vermont.
H. H. F. and A. Lomax, Collectors
November, 1939

Structure: A B A C D E (2,2,2,2½,2,2); Rhythm A; Contour: undulating; Scale: major

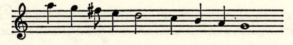

t.c. C.

For mel. rel. see Sharp 1, 281 G.

Anthony Rowley

Tr. H. E. F. B.

There was an old farm-er; he got him a farm.
O fie-lid-dy, fie - lay. There was an old

[2] "began for to rattle" in the retake.

farm-er; he got him a farm, But he hadn't an-y
ox-en to car-ry it on. To me right leg,
left leg, o-ver leg, un-der leg, O-ver old
An-tho-ny Row-ley! So he yoked up a hog and his
broth-er's old cow, O fie-lid-dy, fie-lay. He
yoked up a hog and his broth-er's old cow, And he
car-ried it on as the dev-il knows how.
To me right leg, left leg, o-ver leg, under leg, O-ver old An-tho-ny Row-ley.

Anthony Rowley

There was an old farmer; he got him a farm,
O fie-liddy, fie-lay.
There was an old farmer; he got him a farm,

But he hadn't any oxen to carry it on.
To me right leg, left leg, over leg, under leg,
Over old Anthony Rowley.

(*Follow pattern of first stanza for all stanzas.*)

So he yoked up a hog and his brother's old cow
And he carried it on as the devil knows how.

Oh, the devil he came to the old man one day,
Saying, "One of your family I do crave!"

"Oh," says the old farmer, "I am undone,
For the devil is after my oldest son!"

" 'Tis not your oldest son I crave
But your damn' old scolding wife I must have!"

"Take her, oh, take her with all of my heart
And I hope you two may never part!"

So the old devil he swung her up onto his back
And down to hell's gate went full clickety-clack.

There was a little devil a-mending some chains.
She up with her club and she kicked out his brains.

"Oh," says the old devil, "let's put her up higher."
She up with her club and knocked nine in the fire.

"Oh," says the old devil, "let's put her down lower."
She up with her club and killed nine more.

It was a little devil peeked over hell's wall,
Saying, "Carry her back for she'll kill us all."

And so the old devil he put her in a sack
And like a damn' fool went lugging her back.

"Oh," says the old woman, "I think I've done well.
I've killed nineteen devils and conquered hell."

So you see that the women are worse than the men.
You see that the women are worse than the men.
They'll go through hell and back again.

G

As sung by Jonathan Moses of Orford, New Hampshire.

Alan Lomax, Collector
November, 1939

Structure: A B C D E F (2,2,2,2,2,1½) ; Rhythm A; Contour: approaching an arc; Scale: hexatonic

t.c. G.

For mel. rel. see RO1, 189.

Bonnie Muriley

Tr. M. O.

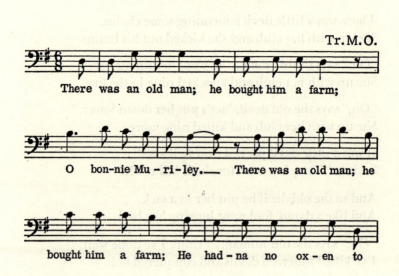

There was an old man; he bought him a farm;

O   bon-nie Mu – ri-ley.___   There was an old man; he

bought him   a farm; He had-na   no   ox-en   to

Bonnie Muriley

There was an old man; he bought him a farm;
O bonnie Muriley.
There was an old man; he bought him a farm;
He hadna no oxen to carry it on.
To my right leg, left leg, over leg, under leg,
Bonnie Muriley.

(Follow pattern of first stanza for all stanzas.)

He yoked up his dog beside the old sow,
Went walloping 'round, the devil knows how.

He saw the old devil on one certain day,
Saying, "One of your family I'll carry away!"

Out cries the old man, "I am undone
For the devil has came for my oldest son!"

"It's not your oldest son," he replied,
"But your old scolding wife I will carry away."

"Oh, take her, oh, take her, with all my heart!
I hope you and she never will part!"

The old devil he swung her acrost his back
And up to hell's glory went clickety-clack.

Oh, when he got her up to hell's door—
For when he got her up to hell's door
He threw her down there—"Lie there, you — !"

He saw a young devil preparing his chains;
She up with her foot and she kicked out his brains.

Another young devil—"Let's hitch her up higher";
She up with her foot and kicked nine in the fire.

Another young devil peeped over the wall;
"Carry off, Master Devil, she will kill us all!"

The old devil he swung her acrost his back
And like a damn' fool he went lugging her back.

He came to the old man who was jogging his plow,
Saying, "Take your old wife for I cannot keep her now."

Out cries the old man, "You're born with a curse.
You've been to hell and you're back—a damn' sight worse!"

H

Recorded from the singing of Mrs. Wallace Baldwin of Springfield, Vermont, who learned this in her childhood days at Twenty-Mile Stream near Cavendish, Vermont.

H. H. F., Collector
May, 1932

The Farmer's Curst Wife

Says the old farmer, "I am undone."
    O, fyliddy, fy lay.
Says the old farmer, "I am undone
For the devil is after my oldest son."
        With her right leg, left leg,
        Over leg, under leg,
        Over Old Anthony Rowley.

" 'Tis not your oldest son I crave,"
      O, fyliddy, fy lay,
"But your damned old scolding wife I must have."
         With her right leg, left leg,
         Over leg, under leg,
         Over Old Anthony Rowley.

(*He carries her off and in hell,*)
She up with her leg and kicked nine in the fire.

(*When he returns her to the farmer comes this ending stanza:*)
They say that the women are worse than the men,
      O, fyliddy, fy lay,
For they go through hell and back again.
         With her right leg, left leg,
         Over leg, under leg,
         Over Old Anthony Rowley.

I

As sung by Charles Ordway of Tunbridge, Vermont. He learned this ballad from his parents.

                         M. Olney, Collector
                         July 29, 1945

Structure: A A B C (4,4,4,4); Rhythm A; Contour: arc; Scale: hexachordal

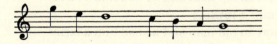

t.c. B flat.

There was an old man and he had him a farm;

O-bree-rant-a-row-ley; There was an old man and he had him a farm; O-bree-rant-a-row-ley; There was an old man and he had him a farm And he had no team to car-ry it on, To my right leg, left leg, up-per leg, un-der leg, O-bree-rant-a-row-ley.

There was an old man and he had him a farm;
O-bree-rant-a-rowley;
There was an old man and he had him a farm;
O-bree-rant-a-rowley;
There was an old man and he had him a farm
And he had no team to carry it on,
To my right leg, left leg, upper leg, under leg,
O-bree-rant-a-rowley.

(Follow pattern of first stanza for all stanzas.)

So he yoked up his dog by the side of his sow,
He yoked up his dog by the side of his sow,
He yoked up his dog by the side of his sow.

The old devil he came to him one day,
Saying, "One of your family I'll take away."

"Pray, it's not my oldest son that you crave;
It's not my oldest son that you crave;
Pray, it's not my oldest son that you crave."

The old devil he took her upon his back
Just like a paddy goes carrying his sack.

J

*Mrs. Delia Welch of Groton, Vermont, sister of Mrs. W. B.
Morton, sang this song, as known to her mother.*

H. H. F., *Collector*
October 19, 1937

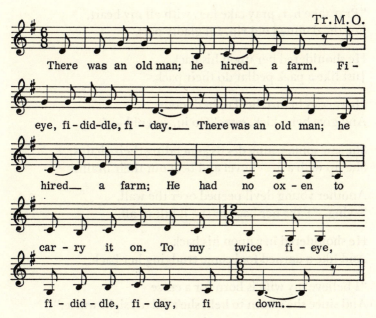

There was an old man; he hired a farm. Fi-
eye, fi-did-dle, fi-day.___ There was an old man; he
hired a farm; He had no ox-en to
car-ry it on. To my twice fi-eye,
fi-did-dle, fi-day, fi down.___

There was an old man; he hired a farm.
Fi-eye, fi-diddle, fi-day.
There was an old man; he hired a farm;
He had no oxen to carry it on.
To my twice fi-eye, fi-diddle, fi-day, fi-down.

(Follow pattern of first stanza for all stanzas.)

He yoked up his hogs in order to plow.
He made a mistake and he yoked his old sow.

The devil he came one certain day,
Saying, "I'm after one of your nice familee."

The old man cries, "I am undone,
For the devil is after my oldest son."

" 'Tis not your oldest son I crave
But 'tis your old scolding wife and she I'll have."

"Pray take her, pray take her, with all my heart,
For the damned old rip, I'll gladly part."

He shouldered her upon his back
Just like a pack pedlar do their pack.

He carries her to the Tophet's door
And give her a kick, says, "Go in, you old —."

She saw some young devils a-mending their chains;
She up with a fire-shovel and beat out their brains.

Another young devil peeped over the wall,
Saying, "Take her back or she'll kill us all."

He shouldered her upon his back
And like a darned fool come trudging her back.

"I believe my wife is born for a curse
And since she's been to hell, she's a darn sight worse."

K

Mrs. A. R. Blake of White River Junction, Vermont, furnished this song as recalled by Mrs. Tryphena A. B. Estabrooks of North Orange, Massachusetts, who lived most of her life at Hardwick, Vermont. Mrs. Estabrooks wrote on her copy, "It's more than 60 years since grandma used to sing it—nearer 65." Grandma was Mrs. Olive Edgerly Sulham of New Hampshire, a descendent of Governor Benning Wentworth. Olive Edgerly's mother was a Wentworth. Mrs. Estabrooks' copy was written about 1925.

H. H. F., Collector
July 31, 1935

The Farmer's Curst Wife

There was an old man, he bought him a farm,
Fli lilla fli lee fli down
There was an old man, he bought him a farm,
And he hadn't any oxen to carry it on.
To my trice fli lilla fli lee fli down.

(Follow pattern of first stanza for all stanzas.)

He yoked up his hogs in order to plough;
The hogs they went, the devil knows how.

The old man cries, "I am undone,
For the devil is after my oldest son."

" 'Tis not your oldest son I crave,
But 'tis your scolding wife I'll have."

"Well, you may take her if you please,
And with her you make take her cheese."

The old devil shouldered her on to his back,
And like a pedlar went hugging his pack.

He carried her down to Tophet's door,
And there he thrashed her on the floor.

He called a little devil to brand him a chain;
She up with her foot and kicked out his brains.

Another little devil that wore a blue cap,
She up with her foot and brained at that.

Another little devil peeked over the wall,
Saying, "Carry her back, or she'll brain us all."

The old devil shouldered her onto his back,
And like a darned fool went carrying her back.

He carried her home to her own door,
And there he thrashed her on the floor,

Saying, "Here's your wife, she's born for a curse,
She has been through hell and she is ten times worse."

L

*As sung by Elmer Barton of Quechee, Vermont. Learned
when a young boy from his uncle, who lived in the northern
part of the state. Published in* Ballads Migrant in New England, *49.*[1]

M. *Olney, Collector*
August 13, 1945

Structure: A[1] B A[2] C D[1] D[2] (2,2,2,2,2,2); Rhythm A; Contour: descending; Scale: hexatonic

[1] On the LP record made in 1953 Mr. Barton omitted Stanza 6, made
minor changes in wording, and added the following stanza at the end:

> Well, the old woman she went yelling all over the hills,
>   Lowland tickle O lay.
> The old woman went yelling all over the hill.
> The devil won't have her 'n' I don't know who will!
>   Saying lowland tickle O laddie,
>   Lowland tickle O lay.

t.c. C.

Farmer's Curst Wife

Tr. M. O.

Farmer's Curst Wife

There was an old man who bought him a farm,
    Saying low-land tick-le O lay.
There was an old man who bought him a farm
And he had no team to carry it on,
    Saying low-land tick-le O laddie,
    Low-land tick-le O lay.

(Follow pattern of the first stanza for all stanzas.)

So he yoked up his dog beside his sow.
He yoked up his dog beside his sow
And he went walloping 'round, the devil knows how.

But he met the old devil on one certain day.
He met the old devil on one certain day,
Saying, "One of your family I'll carry away."

"Oh," out cries the old man, "I am undone!"
Out cries the old man, "I am undone!
The devil has come for my oldest son!"

"No, it is not your son," the devil did say;
" 'Tis not your son," the devil did say,
"But your scolding old wife I'll carry away."

"Oh, take her, oh, take her with all my heart!
Take her, oh, take her with all my heart
And I hope and pray you will never part!"

So the old devil swung her across his back,
The old devil swung her across his back
And up to hell's door he went clickerty-clack.

There was one little devil preparing the chains,
There was one little devil preparing the chains,
While she up with her foot and she kicked out his brains.

Then another little devil said, "Hitch her up higher!"
Another little devil said, "Hitch her up higher!"
For she up with her foot and she kicked nine in the fire.

Then another little devil peeked over the wall,
Another little devil peeked over the wall;
"Carry her back, Master Devil, she will kill us all!"

So the old devil he swung her across his back,
The old devil he swung her across his back
And like a darn fool he went tugging her back.

And the old devil he threwed her down on the floor,
The old devil he threwed her down on the floor,
Saying, "Got to stay here—go to hell no more!"

Then out cried the old man, "You were born for a curse!"
Out cried the old man, "You were born for a curse;
You've been to hell, now you're a whole lot worse!"

M

*Recorded in Wardsboro, Vermont, from the singing of
George Farnham, as learned from E. S. Gale of Millington,
Massachusetts, near Orange. Mr. Gale is the half brother of
Mrs. Josepha Cobb of Londonderry, Vermont, who has given
several songs. Printed in* Vermont Folk-Songs & Ballads, *226.*

George Brown, Collector
August 28, 1930

Structure: A B A C D^c (2,2,2,2,2) ; Rhythm A and B; Contour: undulating; Scale: major

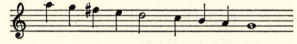

t.c. C.

The Scolding Wife

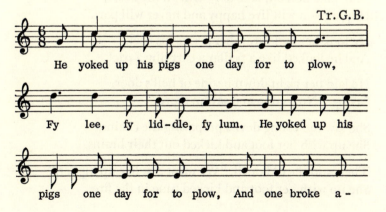

Tr. G.B.

He yoked up his pigs one day for to plow,
Fy lee, fy lid-dle, fy lum. He yoked up his
pigs one day for to plow, And one broke a-

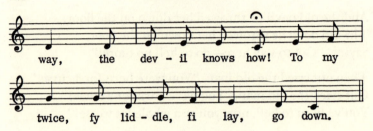

way,   the   dev - il   knows   how!   To   my

twice,   fy   lid - dle,   fi   lay,   go   down.

The Scolding Wife

He yoked up his pigs one day for to plow,
Fy lee, fy liddle, fy lum.
He yoked up his pigs one day for to plow,
And one broke away, the devil knows how!
To my twice, fy liddle, fy lay, go down.

(Follow pattern of first stanza for all stanzas.)

The devil, he came to him one day,
Saying, "One of your family I must take away."

Then says the farmer, "I'm undone,
For the devil has called for my oldest son."

" 'Tis not your oldest son I crave,
But your old scolding wife that I must have."

"Oh, take her, oh, take her, with all my heart,
Hoping you will live happy and never will part."

He took her and threw her across his back
And he looked like a pedlar a-carrying a pack.

He laid her right down beside of hell's door,
Saying, "Now go in and say no more."

She saw the young devils preparing the chains.
She up with her foot and kicked out their brains.

Then said the old devil, "We must cast her up higher."
She up with her foot and kicked nine in the fire.

Then says the old devil, "Must carry her back,
For I believe, on my soul, she would destroy the whole pack."

Then he took her and threw her across his back
And the damned old pedlar came bringing her back.

There's just three things that the devil can't drive—
A hog, and a woman, and bees into a hive.

N

*Mrs. Florence Underhill, with two sisters, the Misses Young
of Bellows Falls, Vermont, remembered this song as sung by
their father, Edward O. Young, uncle of the late Dr. Ellis
of Brookfield, Vermont.*

H. H. F., *Collector*
November 2, 1938

Structure: A B C D (internal repetition) E^d (2,2,2,2,4);
Rhythm A; Contour: undulating; Scale: hexatonic

t.c. G.

For mel. rel. see GCM, 377; Sharp 1, 277 C.

The Scolding Wife

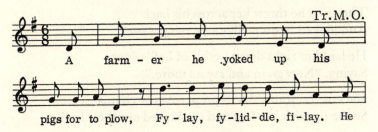

yoked up his pigs one day for to plow And
one broke a-way, the dev-il knows how! With a
twice fy-lay, fy-lid-dle, fy-lay me down.

The Scolding Wife

A farmer he yoked up his pigs for to plow,
Fy-lay, fy-liddle, fy-lay.
He yoked up his pigs one day for to plow
And one broke away, the devil knows how!
With a twice fy-lay, fy-liddle, fy-lay me down.

(Follow pattern of first stanza for all stanzas.)

The devil he came to him one day,
Saying, "One of your family I must take away."

Then said the farmer, "I'm undone,
For the devil has called for my oldest son."

" 'Tis not your eldest son I crave
But your old scolding wife I must have."

"Oh, take her, oh, take her, with all my heart.
I hope you'll live happy and never part."

The devil he threw her across his back
And looked like a pedlar a-carrying a pack.

He laid her right down beside of hell's door,
Saying, "Now go in and say no more."

She saw the young devils preparing the chains
So she up with her foot and she kicked out their brains.

Then said the old devil, "We must cast her up higher."
She up with her foot and kicked nine in the fire.

Then the old devil said, "I must carry her back
For I think, on my soul, she'll destroy the whole pack."

The devil he threw her across his back
And like an old pedlar came bringing her back.

The devil he came to the farmer's door,
Saying, "Take the old scold; I will keep her no more."

The farmer said as they came o'er the hill,
"If the devil won't keep her, I don't know who will."

There are just three things a devil can't drive:
A hog, and a woman, and bees in a hive.

O

Recorded in Townshend, Vermont, from the singing of Josiah S. Kennison, who learned this song from his wife's father, James W. Adams of Johnson, Vermont.

George Brown, Collector
August 25, 1930

Structure: A B¹ A B² Cᵇ (2,2,2,2,2); Rhythm A; Contour: undulating; Scale: hexatonic

t.c. B flat.

The Old Man A-Jogging the Plow

Tr. M. O.

There was an old man a-jog-ging a plow,

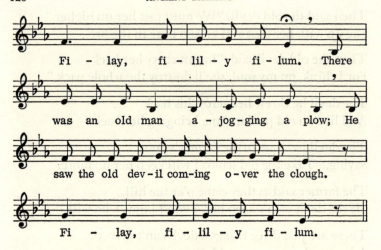

The Old Man A-Jogging the Plow

There was an old man a-jogging a plow,
Fi-lay, fi-lily fi-lum.
There was an old man a-jogging a plow;
He saw the old devil coming over the clough.
Fi-lay, fi-lily fi-lum.

(Follow pattern of first stanza for all stanzas.)

Then cries the old man, "I am undone.
The devil's come after my oldest son."

" 'Tis not your oldest son I crave;
It's your damned old scolding wife I'll have."

Then cries the old man, "Take her with all my heart,
That you and she shall never part."

The old devil he mounted her on his back;
He looked like a pedlar carrying his pack.

He carried her up to the gates of hell
And set her up there and swore she looked well.

She saw the old devil preparing his change;
She up with her foot and kicked out his brains.

The young devils they all began to squall,
Saying, "Carry her back or she'll kill us all."

Then cries the old devil, "Let's mount her up higher,"
And she up with her foot and kicked nine in the fire.

The old devil he mounted her on his back
And like a damned fool went carrying her back.

He carried her to the man a-jogging the plow,
Saying, "Here is your wife; I can't keep her now."

The old woman went swearing all over the hill,
Saying, "If the devil won't keep me I don't know who will."

P

Sung by Mrs. Sarah Lane of Howland, Maine.

M. Olney, Collector
May 11, 1942

The Old Man Hitched up His Hogs to Plow

Oh, the old man hitched up his hogs to plow,
    Fal dal-diddle i-dy-o.
'Twas this way and that way, the devil knows how,
    To my rang-tang fal-diddle i-dy-o.

(Follow pattern of first stanza for all stanzas.)

Oh, the devil came to his plow one day,
Saying, "One of your family I must take away."

"Oh, dear, oh, dear, what shall I do?
Oh, my oldest son I must let go."

"'Tis not your oldest son I crave,
But your darned old scolding wife I'll have."

He put her in an old long sack
And threw her over his old back.

He carried her over a field or moor
And set her down at hell's back door.

One little devil peeked over the wall,
Saying, "Carry her back or she'll kill us all."

He set her over a brimstone pot.
She swore it was almighty hot.

He put her in his old long sack,
And like an old fool went sacking her back.

This shows that women are worse than men,
For they go to hell and back again.

Q

*Sung by Fred Brackett of Stacyville, Maine. This ballad is
an example of how the story was of primary importance to
the singer; the air or meter, of no importance.*

M. Olney, Collector
May 10, 1942

Structure: A¹ B¹ A² B¹ C D A³ B² (2½,2,2,2,2,2,2,2½);
Rhythm A; Contour: approaching an arc; Scale: Mixolydian

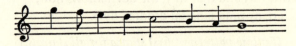

t.c. D.

The Scolding Wife

Tr. H. E. F. B.

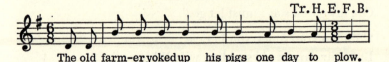

The old farm-er yoked up his pigs one day to plow.

'Twas this way and that way, the dev-il knows how.

The old man was to work in his gar-den one day,

And he spied the old dev-il just o-ver the way.

The old man, he cried, "It's I'm un-done, For it's

my old-est son now that you do crave." "Oh

no, it's not your eld-est son I crave, But your

damned old scold-ing wife, and her I must have."

The Scolding Wife

The old farmer yoked up his pigs one day to plow.
'Twas this way and that way, the devil knows how.
The old man was to work in his garden one day,
And he spied the old devil just over the way.

The old man, he cried, "It's I'm undone,
For it's my oldest son now that you do crave."

"Oh, no, it's not your oldest son I crave,
But your damned old scolding wife, and her I must have."
"Oh, take her, oh, take her," the old devil cries—

The old devil he took her and put her in his pack,
And like a bold soldier he shouldered his sack.
He lugged her along till he come in sight of hell's gates.
He laid her down and opened the door
And then he kicked her in among ten thousand more.
She saw ten little devils a-pickin' up chains;
She rolled up her fist and knocked out nine of their brains.

"Oh, take her away," the little devils they cries,
"For she will kill us all – – –"

The old devil he thought the little devils were setting her up
        higher;
She swung round her leg and kicked nine in the fire.

Oh, the old devil he put her then in his pack
And then like a bold soldier he shouldered his sack.
And now he says that women are worse than the men
For they've been to hell and got safe back again.

*Mr. Brackett's comment: "That's giving the women quite a
hard gouge."*

R

*As sung by Oscar Degreenia of Cornwall, Connecticut. Mr.
Degreenia learned this ballad from his father, who was born
in Barton, Vermont.*

M. Olney, Collector
July 29, 1954

Fie Diddle O-Day

There was an old farmer lived close to hell.
Fie Diddle O-Day.

One morning the farmer went out to plough.
Fie Diddle O-Day.
He saw the old devil come 'cross his plough.
Fie Diddle O-Day.

(Follow same pattern for remaining stanzas.)

"It's not your oldest son I want;
It's your darling wife I'm after now."

"You can have my old woman with all my heart."

He threw the old woman upon his back
And like a damn pedlar went carrying his pack.

And when he got to the gates of hell
Three little devils were climbing the chains.

S

*As sung by J. A. Taggart of Greenfield, Massachusetts,
learned from his Grandmother Pettis.*

H. H. F., *Collector*
October 2, 1939

Structure: A¹ B A² C (2,2,2,3); Rhythm A; Contour: generally descending; Scale: hexachordal

t.c. F.

For mel. rel. see MF, 323.

Fi-Lay   Fi-Little Fi-Lay

Fi-Lay Fi-Little Fi-Lay

There was an old man and he hir-ed a farm.
Fi-lay, fi-little, fi-lay.
He had no oxen to carry it on,
And it's twice fi-lay, fi-little, fi-lay-me down.

He yoked up his horse in order to plough.
Fi-lay, fi-little, fi-lay.
The horse they went until . . .
And it's twice fi-lay, fi-little, fi-lay-me down.

T

As sung by Mrs. A. R. Blake of White River Junction, Vermont.

H. H. F., *Collector*
1935

Structure: A B C D E (2,2,2,2,2); Rhythm A; Contour: approaching an arc; Scale: major

t.c. B flat.

The Farmer's Curst Wife

Tr. M. O.

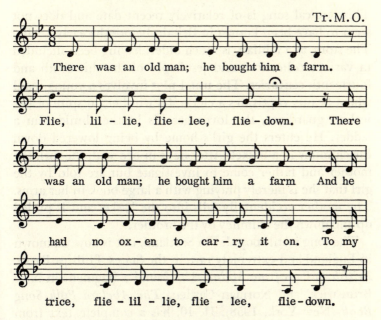

There was an old man; he bought him a farm.

Flie, lil - lie, flie - lee, flie - down. There

was an old man; he bought him a farm And he

had no ox - en to car - ry it on. To my

trice, flie - lil - lie, flie - lee, flie - down.

The Farmer's Curst Wife

There was an old man; he bought him a farm.
   Flie, lillie, flie-lee, flie-down.
There was an old man; he bought him a farm
And he had no oxen to carry it on.
   To my trice, flie-lillie, flie-lee, flie-down.

The Keach i' the Creel

(Child 281)

This farcical song is of relatively recent date and does not seem to have been known in Britain before the early 1800's. The story, as a fabliau, is much older, having been included in various collections and jest-books of the thirteenth and fourteenth centuries. The usual plot involves a young maid whose beauty captivates a clerk. To win her, in spite of her jealous guardians, the lover has his brother build him a ladder. He enters the girl's home by being lowered down the chimney in a basket. After he is in bed with the girl, the mother and father come to investigate but are told by the girl that she is merely praying with a large book in her arms. The mother accidentally falls into the basket and is pulled up and down the chimney by the brother.

The song is still popular in Scotland, but is now unknown in England and extremely rare in the States. Phillips Barry, *British Ballads from Maine,* 336, found a fragment in New Brunswick, and Norman Cazden, *The Abelard Folk Song Book* (New York, 1958), II, 10, has a complete text from New York. The Flanders text gives two of the stanzas that open the story and one in which the mother is tossed about. The roughing up of the mother seems to be the portion of the song that lasts best.

For bibliographical references, of which there are almost none that are not Scottish, see Coffin, 150–1 (American); Dean–Smith, 82 (English); and Greig and Keith, 230–3 (Scottish).

As sung in northern New Hampshire. Name of singer withheld by request.

M. Olney, Collector

Structure: A B C D (2,2,2,2); Rhythm C; Contour: undulating; Scale: hexachordal

t.c. A.

For mel. rel. see possibly BES, 337.

The Keach i' the Creel

Tr. M. O.

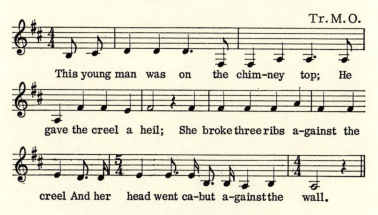

This young man was on the chim-ney top; He gave the creel a heil; She broke three ribs a-gainst the creel And her head went ca-but a-gainst the wall.

The Keach i' the Creel[1]

"How shall I get to your bedroom door?
How shall I get to your bed,
When your father locks his doors at night
And the keys lie under his head?"

"Go get you a ladder nicely made,
Three score feet and three;

[1] keach: catch; creel: basket.

Place it up the chimney top
And down in the creel come to me."

This young man was on the chimney top;
He gave the creel a heil;
She broke three ribs against the creel
And her head went ca-but against the wall.

To my right fal-der rol,
O raddle duddle dull,
And her head went ca-but against the wall.

The Yorkshire Bite

(Laws L 1, similar to Child 283)

"The Crafty Farmer," Child 283, is rare indeed in America, though J. Harrington Cox, *Folk Songs of the South* (Cambridge, Mass., 1925), 166, prints a text close to Child A. In this country, the usual songs of the thief outwitted belong to "The Yorkshire Bite" group. However, there are a number of ballads on the resourcefulness of simple folk in the face of robbery that circulated in the chapbooks and on the broadsheets of the last 250 years, and one called "The Maid of Rygate" (Laws L 2) has also been collected in the New World. Why Child chose one and excluded the others from his select circle is not really clear. In "The Crafty Farmer" the farmer throws an old saddle bag over a hedge and when the thief goes after it rides off on the highwayman's horse. In "The Yorkshire Bite" a boy spreads money on the grass and when the thief dismounts to get it rides off on the highwayman's horse. And in "The Maid of Rygate" a girl, stripped naked by a thief, outwits him and rides off on his horse. All three are much alike in age and quality, as well as in plot. For that matter, "The Yorkshire Bite" and "The Maid of Rygate" go back at least to 1769 when they appeared in *Logan's Pedlar's Pack*, 131 and 133 respectively. "The Crafty Farmer" has not been traced before 1796.

A bite is a shrewd trick played on a dull-witted person—like those tricks for which the Yorkshiremen were famous. Vermonters, see Flanders J, evidently felt New Hampshiremen were capable of similar shrewdness.

The Flanders versions are much of a kind and quite like other American texts. For a bibliography to "The Crafty Farmer," "The Yorkshire Bite," and "The Maid of Rygate" in America, see Coffin, 151–2. "The Crafty Farmer" is listed in Dean–Smith, 102 (English) and in Greig and Keith, 236–7 (Scottish). "The Yorkshire Bite" is in Dean–Smith, 55 (English), while that song, and "The Maid of Rygate" are in Laws *ABBB*, 165–6, under L 1 and L 2 (British and American). See also Child, V, 128–31, for a discussion.

On March 2, 1948, the following story, copied from *The Farmer's Almanac* for 1860, was sent to Mrs. Flanders by George E. Smith of Takoma Park, Maryland. It bears a striking resemblance to all three ballads and was evidently reprinted from a daily newspaper, *The Pennsylvanian*, once published in Philadelphia.

The Farmer's Daughter and the Robber

A farmer living a few miles from Easton, sent his daughter on horse back to that town, to procure from the bank smaller notes in exchange for one hundred dollars. When she arrived there, the bank was shut, and she endeavored to effect her object by offering at several stores, but could not get her note changed. She had not gone far on her return, when a stranger rode to the side of her horse and accosted her with so much politeness, that she had not the slightest suspicion of any evil intent on his part. After riding a mile or two, employed in very social conversation, they came to a very retired part of the road, and the gentleman commanded her to give him the bank note. It was with some difficulty that she could be made to believe him in earnest, as his demeanor had been very friendly; but the presentation of a pistol placed the matter beyond a doubt, and she yielded to necessity. Just as she held the note to him, a sudden puff of wind blew it into the road, and carried it gently several yards from them. The discourteous knight alighted to overtake it, and the lady whipped her horse to get out of his power, and the other horse which had been left standing by her side, started off with her. His owner fired a pistol, which only tended to increase the speed of all parties—and the lady arrived safely at home with the horse of the robber, on which was a pair of saddle bags. When these were opened, they were found to contain, besides a quantity of counterfeit bank notes, fifteen hundred dollars in good money! The horse was a good one, and when saddled and bridled was thought to be worth as much at least as the bank note that was stolen.

All of the tunes for Child 283 are related, and can be sub-divided into three groups: (1) Britton, Brooks, Harvey, Davis, Moore, and Williams; (2) Edwards, Merrill; and (3) Moses. Related tunes, and, indeed, tunes for this ballad in any relationship, were extremely hard to find. For the Britton group, see FCB4 p. 119, No. 46, for general relationship.

A

As sung by Mrs. Laura Britton of Putney, Vermont. Learned from her mother, Jennie Sleeper, who was born in Chelsea, Vermont.

H. H. F., Collector, April 15, 1943
Retake by M. Olney
January 8, 1945

Structure: A¹ A² Bª C D (2,2,2,2,2½); Rhythm D; Contour: arc; Scale: Aeolian

t.c. D.

The Yorkshire Boy

Tr. H. E. F. B.

In Lon-don there lived a ma-son by trade, Who had for his serv-ants a man and a maid; An 'Ork-shire boy, a clev-er man to fend, To do his mas-ter's busi-ness, his name was John. Fol-de-rol, day-did-dle-dol, fol-de-rol-de-dy.

The Yorkshire Boy

In London there lived a mason by trade,
Who had for his servants a man and a maid;
An 'orkshire boy, a clever man to fend,
To do his master's business, his name was John.
Fol-de-rol, day-diddle-dol, fol-de-rol-de-day.

One morning early he call-ed to his John;
John hearing master, quickly he run,
"You take my cow and drive her to the fair
For she's in good order and it's all I have to spare."

(Repeat refrain after each stanza.)

Jack taking the cow, 'twas out of the barn
And started for the fair, as you may learn;
In about ten miles he met with a man
Who bought his cow, paid him the money, six pound and ten.

He called in a tavern for to take a drink
And all that he called for he paid down the chink;
When unto the landlady thus he did say:
"For what shall I do with my money, I pray?"

"I will sew it up in your coat lining," said she,
"Least robbed on the highway you may be."
The robber stood behind, a-drinking of his wine,
And he said to himself, "That money's all mine!"

Jack taking the leave and off he did go,
The robber following after him also;
He overtook the boy—'twas in the highway—
"It's well overtaken, young man!" said he.

"How far are you going, young man?" said he.
"Jump right up behind me and I'll be your company—
About ten miles, as near as I know."
So Jack jumped behind him and away they go.

They rode on for a space of a mile,
Talking very civil for a while,
When unto Jack the robber he did say,
"Deliver up your money or your life I'll take away!"

Jack seeing it no time to dispute or to doubt,
So out of his coat lining the money he drew out;
So out of his coat lining the money he drew out
And into the dirt he strewed it well about.

The robber getting down off from his horse,
Thinking very little it would be for his loss,
And while he was picking the money that Jack strewed,
Jack jumped a horseback and away he rode.

The robber advised Jack for to stay
But Jackie never minded and straight he rode away;
When unto his master thus he did bring
A saddle, a bridle, and many fine things.

The old man coming out of his door
To meet his little servant-boy he often had before,
Being astonished and looking very cross,
He says, "What in the devil's my old cow turned to a horse?"

"Oh, no, my good master, your cow I have sold,
And it was robbed on the highway by the highwayman bold;
While he was picking the money that I strewed,
I jumped a horseback and away I rode."

The saddle bags were taken and out of them were told
Five hundred bright guineas all in solid gold,
Besides a pair of pistols; and Jack says he, "I vow,
I think, my good master, I've well sold your cow!"

The old man says, "I vow and declare,
Three quarters of this money shall be for your share,
And as for the villing I think you served him right;
I think you put upon him a true Yorkshire Bite!"

B

As sung by Asa Davis of Milton, Vermont. Learned from his father, Joel Davis. Published in Ballads Migrant in New England, *51.*

H. H. F., Collector
November 8, 1945

Structure: A A B C D (4,4,4,4,4); Rhythm D but divergent;
Contour: arc; Scale: hexatonic

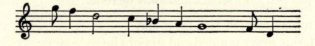

t.c. C.

The Yorkshire Boy

Tr. M. O.

In Lon-don there liv-ed a ma-son by
trade. He had him two serv-ants, a man and a
maid. The York-shire boy he had for his man And to
do his busi-ness, his name it was John. Tim-i
fol, dol-di-lie-do, fol lol-der day.

The Yorkshire Boy

In London there liv-ed a mason by trade.
He had him two servants, a man and a maid.
The Yorkshire boy, he had for his man
And to do his business, his name it was John.

Timi fol, dol-di-lie-do, fol lol-der day.[1]
'Twas early one morning he called his man John.
John hearing his master unto him did run,
Says, "Take this cow and drive her to the fair,
For she is cross and she hooked my old mare."

(*Repeat refrain after each stanza.*)

John he took the cow all out of the barn,
And drove her to the fair, as we do learn,

[1] In a second singing the same day, Mr. Davis gave this refrain:
Lol de trol lol trol lol trol de dol der day.

And then pretty soon he met some men
And sold them the cow for six pounds, ten.

He went to the tavern to get him some drink,
For the good old farmers paid him down the chink.
He went to the landlady and thus he did say,
"Oh, what shall I do with my money, I pray?"

"All in your coat lining I'll sew it up," she said,
"For fear that on the highway robbed you may be."
The highwayman sat[2] behind a drinking of wine,
And he said to himself, "That money is all mine."

John took his leave and away he did go.
The highwayman followed after his also.
He overtook the boy well on the highway.
"You're well overtaken, young man," he did say.

They went till they came to the long, dark lane.
The highwayman said to the boy, "I'll tell you all plain.
Deliver up your money without fear or strife
Or here in this place I will end your sweet life."

John, seeing no room for any dispute,
Put his hand in his coat lining and pulled the money out;
Out of his coat lining he pulled the money out,
And in the tall grass he strew it all about.

The highwayman getting down from his horse,
But little did he think it was for his loss.
While he was picking money up that was strewed,
John mounted on his horse and away he rode.

The highwayman followed after him for to stay.
John minded nothing about him but still rode away.
Home to his master he did bring
Horse, saddle and bridle and many things.

[2] "sit" in a second singing the same day.

The maid saw the boy as he was returning home
And for to tell his master went in the other room.
The old man came to the door and he said, "What a fox!
Has my old cow turned into a hoss?"

"Oh, no, my good master, your cow I have sold,
Being robbed on the highway by the highwayman bold.
While he was picking money up that I strewed,
I mounted on his horse and away I rode."

The saddle bags being opened as I've been told,
Five hundred pounds of silver and gold,
Besides a pair of pistols. Says John says he, "I vow,
I think, my good old master, I've well sold your cow."

"I think for a boy you have done very rare.
Three quarters of this money you shall have for your share;
And as for the old villain you have served him just right,
For you have put upon him the sure Yorkshire Bite."

C

As sung by Edwin Day of Colebrook, New Hampshire. This ballad was learned as a child from a neighbor who was born in England.

M. Olney, Collector
November 21, 1941

The Yorkshire Boy

In London there lived a mason by trade;
He had for his servant a man and a maid;
A Yorkshire boy he had for his man
And for to do his business; his name it was John.
Lud-li ding-dum tra-la-la,
Tra-la diddle-O-day.

He got up in the morning, called on his man John;
John hearin' his master's voice, so quickly he did run;

"O John, take this cow and lead her to the fair,
For she is in good order; she's all we have to spare."

(Repeat refrain after each stanza.)

Oh, John took the cow all out of the barn
And started for the fair as we do learn.
He hadn't gone far before he met a man.
He sold off his cow for a six pound ten.

He called to the tavern for to get a drink,
While the old landlord was counting out his chink.
He went to the landlady and to her did say,
"What shall I do with my money, I do pray?"

"Oh, in your cut lining sew-ed it shall be,
For fear of a highwayman most robbed you will be."
Highwayman sat behind him drinking up his wine;
He said to himself, "John's money is all mine."

Oh, John took his leaf and away he did go;
The highwayman followed after also.
He overtook John all on the highway.
"You're now overtook, young man," he did say.

He said to this boy, "Won't you jump on and ride?"
"How far are you going?" then Johnny replied.
"About four miles as far as I do know."
And Johnny jumped behind him and away they did go.

They rode till they came to some dark lane.
The highwayman says, "I'll tell you now in plain.
Deliver up your money without any strife,
For in this lonely valley I will take away your life."

Oh, John seeing there was no time for dispute,
He jumped off the hoss without any doubt
And out of his lining the money he poured out;
Along through the tall grass he strewed it well about.

The highwayman jumped all off from his hoss
But little did he think it was for his loss,
And while he was picking up the money John had strewed,
Johnny jumped a-horseback and away he did go.

Highwayman followed after and bid him to stay
But Johnny never minded; still he rode away.
The maid stood in the door; seeing John come home,
She went and told the master who was in the other room.

He came to the door and says to him thus:
"John, has my cow turned into a hoss?"
"Oh, no, my good master, your cow I have sold,
And I have been robbed by a highwayman bold."

They took off the saddlebags and all of them told
Five hundred pounds in silver and gold,
Beside a pair of pistols; and John says, "I vow
I think, my good master, I've well sold your cow."

"Oh, as for a boy, you have done quite well;
Two thirds of this money you shall have for your share;
And as for the villin, you have served him just right;
I guess he'll think it's a Yorkshire Bite."

D

Recorded in Burlington, Vermont, as sung by George Edwards who said, "The Yorkshire Bite was sung by my grandfather, Sergeant William H. Edwards, at St. Jean's Farm, furthest outpost towards the French troops, the evening before the battle of Waterloo. Men were singing either together or separately; his grandfather sang this as a solo. His grandfather had originally been a seaman. He spent three years in the army and then returned to the sea, voyaging, late in life, to Quebec, and settling there." Published in

Country Songs of Vermont, *26, and in* The New Green
Mountain Songster, *97.*

H. H. F., Collector
October 9, 1933

Structure: A B¹ᵃ B² C Dᵃ (4,4,4,4,4); Rhythm C and D; Contour: arc; Scale: Aeolian

t.c. E.

The Yorkshire Bite

Tr. H. E. F. B.

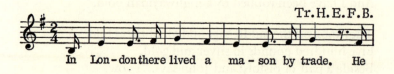

In Lon-don there lived a ma-son by trade. He

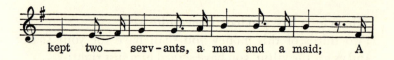

kept two — serv-ants, a man and a maid; A

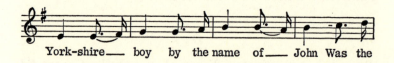

York-shire — boy by the name of — John Was the

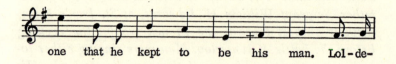

one that he kept to be his man. Lol-de-

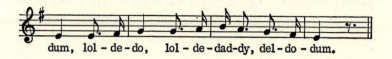

dum, lol-de-do, lol-de-dad-dy, del-do-dum.

The Yorkshire Bite

In London there lived a mason by trade;
He kept two servants, a man and a maid.
A Yorkshire boy by the name of John
Was the one that he kept to be his man.
   Lol-de-dum, lol-de-do, lol-de-daddy, del-do-dum.

One morning so early he called for John;
Johnnie heard his master and quickly he did run
"Take a cow from the barn and go drive her to the fair.
She is in very good order and she's all I have to spare."

  (*Repeat refrain after each stanza.*)

John took the cow and started for the fair,
And on the highway he met three men,
And on the highway he met three men,
And he sold them the cow for six pounds ten.

And then to the tavern, for something to drink;
While the landlord was counting the chink,
Unto the landlady he did say,
"Where shall I put my money, good woman, I pray?"

"In the lining of your coat, sir," she did say,
"Lest by some highwayman, robbed you should be."
There sat a highwayman drinking up his wine;
Thinks he to himself, "This money is all mine."

Then John started off; not far had he gone
When he was overtaken by this same man.
"You are well overtaken, young man," he cried,
"And now along with me won't you jump up and ride?"

"How far are you going this way?" said John.
"Two or three miles, so far as I know,
Two or three miles, so far as I know."
Then up jumped John and away they did go.

They rode along together till they came to a dark lane.
"Now," said this bold robber, "I will tell you in plain.
Deliver up your money without any strife
Or in this lonesome valley I will end your pleasant life."

Then John's not having long to dispute,
From his coat lining he quickly pulled it out,
From his coat lining he quickly pulled it out
And in the tall grass he strewed it about.

The bold robber not thinking of his loss
Began to pick it up and to put it in his purse,
Began to pick it up and to put it in his purse,
While at the same time John rode off on his horse.

The old man called out for John to stay,
But John never minded and still he rode away,
Until he came to his own master's home;
Then horse, saddle, bridle and all was his own.

The portmonie was searched and there was found
Three hundred bright guineas in silver and gold,
A brace of pistols; "I do vow
I think that my master quite well sold his cow."

"Then, Johnnie, for a boy you have done quite rare.
Two thirds of this money you shall have for your share
And as for the rogue, you served him just right—
I think you played him up a fair Yorkshire Bite."

E

Sung by Ainslie B. Lawrence of St. Albans, Vermont, as formerly sung by George Washington Brooks of Sherbrooke, Quebec, to his seventeen children. Written from memory, as given to Ainslie B. Lawrence by his mother, Bella B. Lawrence, and his aunt, Emily Brooks, as they remembered their father, G. W. Brooks, having sung it many years ago. Mr. Brooks was an old-time singing-master. Regarding

Grandfather Brooks, Mr. Lawrence wrote: "He was born in Worcester, Massachusetts, and moved to Sherbrooke, Quebec, where he became a merchant. He owned a 600-acre farm about five miles down the St. Francis River which later became known as Capleton Mines (copper). It was here that most of the children were born. He used to keep a cobbler the year around to make the shoes for the family and the hired help, as well as making harnesses for use on the farm. He also was a builder of highways. I have an old record book of his which dates back to 1826, which shows the cost of labor and materials in connection with his road-building. Three of my uncles were builders of railroads, and one a mining engineer in the West. About the time of the Civil War it became rumored around Sherbrooke that George Brooks was going to head *an army from the U. S. and 'take' Canada. Things got so hot at one time that he had to go into hiding for fear of being killed. Of course there was nothing to it at all. Things quieted down after a spell and he came out into the sunlight once again."* Copied literatim et punctatim, tune as well as text.

H. H. F., Collector
September 16, 1956 [1]

Structure: A A B C D (2,2,2,2,3); Rhythm D but dotted; Contour: arc; Scale: Aeolian, then major

t.c. first D, then F.

The Yorkshire Boy

In London there lived a mason by trade,
Who had for his servants, a man and a maid,

---

[1] A tape recording sent April 19, 1957, differed only slightly from the text above.

The Yorkshire Boy

Tr. A. B. L.

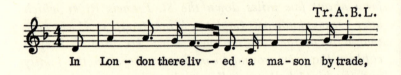

In Lon - don there liv - ed a ma-son by trade,

Who had for his serv-ants a man and a maid,

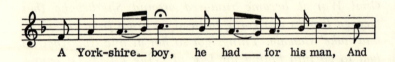

A York-shire boy, he had for his man, And

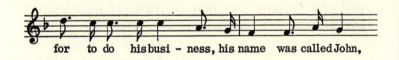

for to do his busi - ness, his name was called John,

Lul de dum lul de did ul lul de

di do lul de did-ul-o day.

A Yorkshire boy, he had for his man,
And for to do his business, his name was called John.

Chorus: Repeat after each verse
Lul de dum lul de did ul lul de di do lul de did-ul-o day.

'Twas early one morning he called his man, John,
Who hearing from his master unto him did run,
"You take this cow and drive her to the fair,
For she's in good order and all that I can spare."

John he took the cow all out of the barn,
And drove her to the fair, as we do learn,
And then pretty soon, he met up with some men
And sold to them the cow for six pounds and ten.

He went to the tavern to get him some drink,
For the good old farmers paid him down the chink.
He went to the landlady and to her he did say,
"Oh! What shall I do with my money, I pray?"

"All in your coat lining I'll sew it," she said,
"For fear on the highway that robbed you may be."
The highwayman sat behind a-drinking wine,
And he said to himself, "That money's all mine."

John took his leave and away he did go,
The highwayman followed after him also,
He overtook the boy well on the highway,
"You're well overtaken, young man," he did say.

They went till they came to the long, dark lane,
The highwayman said, "I'll tell you all plain.
Deliver up your money without fear or strife
Or here in this place I'll end your sweet life."

John seeing no room for any dispute,
Put his hand into his coat lining and pulled the money out,
Out of his coat lining he pulled the money out
And in the tall grass he strew it all about.

The highwayman getting down from off his horse,
Little a-thinking 'twas all for his loss.
While he was picking money up that was well strewed,
John mounted on his horse and away he rode.

The highwayman called after him for to stay.
John minded nothing 'bout him, but still rode away,
And home to his master, he did bring
A horse and saddle and bridle and many other things.

The maid saw the boy as he came riding back home,
And for to tell his master, went in the other room.
The old man came to the door and there he did say,
"What a pox! Has my old cow turned into a horse?"

"Oh no, my good master, your cow I well sold,
Was robbed on the highway by a robber bold.
While he picked the money up that I had strewed,
I jumped onto his horse and away I rode."

The saddle bags were opened, as I have been told,
Five hundred pounds of silver and gold,
Besides a pair of pistols. Says John, "I vow,
I think, my good old master, I've well sold your cow."

"I think for a boy you have done very rare,
Three quarters of this money you'll have for your share
And as for the villain, you served him just right,
For you have put upon him the sure Yorkshire Bite."

F

Mrs. Fred P. Lord of Hanover, New Hampshire, loaned for copying a manuscript in the family heritage of the Rogers family, formerly of Plymouth, New Hampshire, now of Long Beach, California. Among early forebears was Peabody Nathaniel Rogers, a graduate of Dartmouth in 1816, who became a lawyer and an abolitionist in Concord, where he published a paper called The Herald. *Because of his independent views, he and his family were ostracized in the community; he excommunicated the church in Concord! These songs were taught either by the mother from Pennsylvania, Ruth Dodd Luellen, or the father, Daniel Farrand Rogers,*

who may have learned them from his father, Peabody Na-
thaniel Rogers, born in 1794.

H. H. F., Collector

The Yorkshire Bite

In London there lived a mason by trade
Who had for his two servants, a man and a maid;
A Yorkshire boy he had for his man
For to do his business, his name it was Joem.
Tumma-rumpa-toodle-oh-tum
Ti-teedle-eedle-odle-umpa-toodle-oh-tum
Ti-teedle-oh-day.

One day he did call to his man Jack,
Jack hearing his master, quick did he come there.
"Come and take this cow, and drive it to the fair,
For she is in good order and all that I can spare.
Tumma-rumpa . . . *etc.*

The boy took the cow right out of the barn,
For to drive her to the fair, as we're to understand,
But on his way he met three men
To whom he sold the cow for six pounds ten.
Tumma-rumpa . . . *etc.*

They rid to the tavern for to get some drink,
And there the good old farmers paid him down the chink,
Jack spoke to the landlady, and thus he did say:
"What will I do with my money, I pray?"
Tumma-rumpa . . . *etc.*

"Sew it up in your coat lining," the landlady said she:
"For fear upon the highway a-robbed you may be,"
A robber sat behind him a-drinking of his wine,
Says he to himself, "that money's all mine."
Tumma-rumpa . . . *etc.*

The boy took his leave and away he did go,
The highway man followed him also;
At length he overtook him while on the highway,
"Ha! Well overtaken, young man," he did say.
Tumma-rumpa . . . *etc.*

The robber he asked Jack to get up and ride,
"How far are you going?" Jack, he replied.
"About four miles, for what I don't know."
So he jumped up behind him and away they did go.
Tumma-rumpa . . . *etc.*

They rid till they came to a very dark lane,
Says the robber to Jack, "I will tell you in plain,
Deliver up your money without fear or strife,
Or certainly I will take a sweet life."
Tumma-rumpa . . . *etc.*

Jack seeing there was no time for dispute,
Jumped off from behind him without fear or doubt
And from his coat lining, the money he tore out
And in the tall grass, he strewed it all about.
Tumma-rumpa . . . *etc.*

The robber he jumped right off of his hoss,
Never thinking what 'twould be to his loss;
For while he was picking the money that was strowed,
Jack up a-horseback and away he rode.
Tumma-rumpa . . . *etc.*

The robber he called to Jack for to stay,
But Jack never minded and still he rode away,
And home to his master the horse he did bring,
Saddle and bride and marry a fine thing.
Tumma-rumpa . . . *etc.*

The maid seeing Jack come home so soon
To quaint her master ran into the room.

The master he came out and then he spoke thus:
"What you fox, has my cow turned into a hoss?"
Tumma-rumpa . . . *etc.*

"Oh no, my good master, your cow I have sold,
But was robbed on the way by a highwayman bold;
But while he was putting the money in his purse,
To make you amends, I rid off his hoss."
Tumma-rumpa . . . *etc.*

The saddle bags were opened and the money all told,
Five thousand pounds in silver and in gold;
Besides a pair of pistoles, the boy said, "Now,
I think my good master, I've well sold your cow."
Tumma-rumpa . . . *etc.*

"I think, for a boy, you've done very rare,
Three parts of the money shall be to your share;
And as for the villain, you served him just right,
For you gave him the true Old Yorkshire Bite."
Tumma-rumpa . . . *etc.*

G

Mrs. J. W. Davies, Librarian of the Waterford (Vermont)
Free Public Library, shares from its files this song as pre-
sented by Euclid I. Williams of Lower Waterford, Vermont.
He writes, "I was born in 1859; my father, John W. Wil-
liams, was born in 1813, and I learned the song from him
when I was a small boy. My grandfather, John Williams,
was born in 1776, and my father learned the song from him.
My great-grandfather, Williams Williams, came from Wales
when a young man and he learned the song from him, in
Wales." Copied literatim. Printed in the Springfield, Mass.,
Republican, *January 1, 1933. The tune is transcribed as sung*
by his son, L. D. Williams, in 1957.

H. H. F., Collector
Early 1930's

Structure: A¹ A² B C D (4,4,4,4,4); Rhythm D but divergent;
Contour: arc; Scale: hexatonic

t.c. E.

The Yorkshire Bite

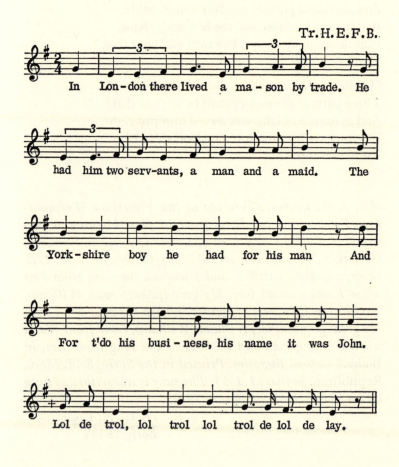

The Yorkshire Bite

In London there lived a mason by trade,
He had him two servants, a man and a maid,
The Yorkshire boy, he had for his man,
And for to do his business, his name it was John.

Lol de trol, lol trol lol trol de lol der day.

Twas early one morning he called his man John,
John hearing his master unto him did run,
Says take this cow and drive her to the fair,
For she is cross and she hooked my old mare. *Chorus:*

John he took the cow all out of the barn
And drove her to the fair, as we do learn,
And then pretty soon, he met some men
And sold them the cow for six pounds, ten. *Chorus:*

He went to the Tavern to get him some drink,
For the good old farmers paid him down the chink,
He went to the landlady and thus he did say,
Oh what shall I do with my money, I pray. *Chorus:*

All in your coat lining I'll sew it up she said,
For fear that on the highway robbed you may be,
The highwayman sit behind a drinking of wine,
And he said to himself that money is all mine. *Chorus:*

John took his leave and away he did go,
The highwayman followed after him also,
He overtook the boy well on the highway,
You're well overtaken young man he did say. *Chorus:*

They went till they came to the long dark lane,
The highwayman said to the boy, I'll tell you all plain
Deliver up your money without fear or strife
Or here in this place I will end your sweet life. *Chorus:*

John seeing no room for any dispute,
Put his hand in his coat lining and pulled the money out
Out of his coat lining he pulled the money out,
And in the tall grass he strew it all about. *Chorus:*

The highwayman getting down from his horse
But little did he think it was for his loss,
While he was picking money up that was strewed,
John mounted on his horse and away he rode. *Chorus:*

The highwayman followed after, him for to stay.
John minded nothing about him, but still rode away.
Home to his master, he did bring
Horse, saddle and bridle and many things. *Chorus:*

The maid saw the boy as he was returning home,
And for to tell his master went in the other room,
The old man came to the door and he said what a fox,
Has my old cow turned into a hoss. *Chorus:*

Oh no my good master, your cow I have sold,
Being robbed on the highway by the highwayman bold,
While he was picking money up that I strewed,
I mounted on his horse and away I rode. *Chorus:*

The saddle bags being opened as I've been told,
Five hundred pounds of silver and gold,
Besides a pair of pistols says John says he I vow,
I think my good old master I've well sold your cow. *Chorus:*

I think for a boy you have done very rare,
Three quarters of this money you shall have for your share
And as for the old villain you have served him just right,
For you have put upon him the sure Yorkshire bite.

Lol de trol lol trol lol trol de dol de day.

H

*As sung by Alonzo Lewis, who was born in the Agamenticus
Section of York, Maine. He learned this song as a young
boy.*

M. *Olney, Collector*
October 1, 1948

In London There Did Dwell

In London there liv-ed a mason by trade,
And for to do his work he'd a man and a maid.
A Yorkshire boy he had for his man
And his name it was John.
And it dol dol lol, addle-da-do.

He woke up one morning; he hollered for John.
Johnnie heard his master, and quickly did run.
"You take this cow and you drive her to the fair
For she's in good order and all I have to spare."
And it dol dol lol, addle-da-do.

Johnnie took his leaf and away he did go.
You'll rob a . . .

Johnnie drove the cow just as fur as he did run;
Before he got tired he met with a man
That paid him all the money, it was six pound and ten
And it dol dol addle and the do.

He call-ed to the tavern to get him a drink;
He owed the old farmer and he paid him all the chink.
To the landlady crying, and thus he did say,
"And what shall I do with my money, I pray?"

"I'll sew it to your coat lining," the fair maid did say,
"Although you may be robbed along the highway."

There sat the robber a-drinking of his wine,
Saying to himself, "Oh, that money is all mine."

And Johnnie took his leaf and away he did go.
The old robber followed after also.
He overtook him all on the highway.
" 'Tis well overtaken, young man," he did say.

" 'Tis won't you get on behind me and ride?"
"How far are you going?" the boy he replied.
"About four miles as for I do know."
Johnnie he jumped on and away they did go.

They rode till they came to some narrow dark lane.
"Now," said the robber, "I'll tell you in plain.
Deliver up your money without stir or strife
Or in the lonesome valley I'll surely take your life."

Johnnie jumped right off without any doubt;
From his coat lining he pulled the money out.
From his coat lining he pulled the money out
And among the tall grass where he stood all about.

The old robber jumped right off, right off from his horse.
Little did he think it would be for his loss.
While picking up his money and putting in his purse,
Johnnie jumped right on and came off with his horse.

The old robber followed after him; he ordered him to stay.
Johnnie never minded; he still rode away.
Home to this master, he did bring
Horse and saddle and many fine things.

The maid seen Johnnie returning home,
She run to her master in the other room.
He come to the door, a-looking very cross,
"How the devil my cow has turned to a horse!"

"Oh, yes, kind sir, your cow I've sold,
And I've been robbed by the highwayman bold;
While picking up his money and putting in his purse
To obey your commands, I come off with his horse.

"The bags I took off . . .
Five hundred pounds in silver and gold
Beside a pile of pistols
Master, I do think . . ."

I

As sung by Charles Wade of Wallingford, Vermont. Mr. Wade learned this song some seventy years ago in his home.
H. H. F., *Collector*
October 3, 1934

The Yorkshire Bite

'Twas early one morning, they call-ed for John.
So quick-lie to his master he come,
Saying, "Take this cow and drive her to the fair
For she's in good order and she we can spare."

Refrain: Tum a toodle, all the dy dle lol
Y dum dum toodle all the day.

The boy took the cow and he drove her from the barn.
He drove her to the fair as we do understand.
He had not gone far 'fore he met two men
And he sold 'em his cow for six pound ten.

(Repeat refrain after each stanza.)

The boy took the money and home he did go,
The highwayman after him also.
They had not gone far 'fore he came up to him,
Saying, "It's well overtaken all on the highway."

"How fur are you going?" the highwayman says.
"How fur are you going?" The boy he replied,
"Three or four miles further on I know."
And they jumped up the horseback and away they did go.

They rode till they came to a dark lane
And then says the driver, "I tell you plain,
Deliver up your money without any strife
Or in this lane I shall end your life."

The boy, seeing no time for to spare,
He leaped from his horse without any doubt;
From his coat lining the money he pulled out,
And in the tall grass he strewed it about.

"And the highwayman leaping from his horse—
All knowing it being for his loss—
Before he had gathered the money that I strowed
I jumped up a-horseback and off I rode."

It was aye but now when John came riding home
Being in to acquaintance he went into the room.
The master in the corner, looking very cross,
Says, "The devil take my cow, turned it into a hoss."

"Oh, no, good master, your cow I have sold,
But I've been robbed of a highwayman bold.
Before he could gather the money that I strowed
I jumped up a-horseback and off I rode."

They opened up the saddle and in it they found
Gold and silver, thousands of pounds.

. . . .

. . . .

The old man laughs and John says, "I vow,
I think, good master, I've well sold your cow."
"Upon this robber you served him just right.
Upon him you put a Yorkshire Bite."

J

Miss May Louise Harvey of Woodstock, Vermont, sang this as learned from her mother, Rebecca Greenough, who came in 1853 to Vermont after her marriage. This was sung by Mrs. Greenough's grandmother, Mrs. Rebecca Hoyt who lived near Concord, New Hampshire, when Mrs. Greenough was a child.

H. H. F., *Collector*
April 26, 1935

Structure: A A B C D E (2,2,2,2,2,2); Rhythm D; Contour: arc; Scale: Aeolian, then Mixolydian

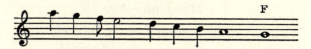

t.c. C, then B flat.

Hampshire Bite

Tr. M. O.

There liv - ed in Lon-don a ma- son by trade;

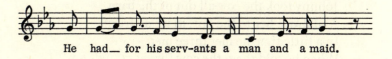

He had— for his serv-ants a man and a maid.

A Hamp-shire boy he had for his man And

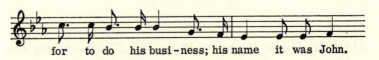

for   to   do   his busi-ness; his name   it was John.

Lol - de-dol,   lol - de-dol, trod - dle all,

Lol - de-dol - de did - dle   all   de   day.

Hampshire Bite

There liv-ed in London a mason by trade.
He had for his servants a man and a maid.
A Hampshire boy he had for his man
And for to do his business; his name it was John.
Lol-de-dol, lol-de-dol, troddle all,
Lol-de-dol-de diddle all de day.

One morning so early he call-ed for John.
John hearing his voice so quickly did come.
"Take this cow, John; drive her to the fair
For she's in good order and all we have to spare."

(Repeat refrain after each stanza.)

Johnny took the cow all out of the barn
And drove her to the fair, as we do learn.
In a little time he met three men
When he sold them the cow for six pounds ten.

They went into a tavern all for to take a drink
And then the old farmer paid him all the chink.
He spoke to the landlady and this he did say,
"And what shall I do with my money, I pray?"

K

*Recorded in Plymouth, Vermont, from the singing of Mrs.
Herbert Moore, learned from her mother, Mrs. Eleanor
(Goff) Benham, born in Brome, Quebec. Mrs. Benham's
father also sang this song. He was Mr. Bamet Goff. The
latter's father came from England, from what part Mrs.
Moore does not know. Published in* Vermont Folk-Songs &
Ballads, *234.*

George Brown, Collector
October 10, 1930

Structure: A¹ A² B C D E (4,4,4,4,4,4); Rhythm D; Contour:
arc; Scale: major, with modulations

t.c. C at beginning and end, F and B flat medially.

The Yorkshire Bite

The boy took the cow· by the horn with his hand

To lead her to the fair, as you may· un - der -

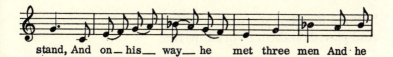

stand, And on— his— way— he met three men And· he

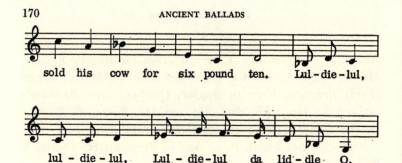

sold his cow for six pound ten. Lul - die - lul,

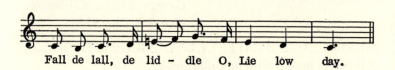

lul - die - lul, Lul - die - lul da lid - dle O,

Fall de lall, de lid - dle O, Lie low day.

The Yorkshire Bite

The boy took the cow by the horn with his hand
To lead her to the fair, as you may understand,
And on his way he met three men,
And he sold his cow for six pound ten.
Lul-die-lul, lul-die-lul,
Lul-die-lul da liddle O,
Fall de lall, de liddle O,
Lie low day.

(*Song of a boy went to market with cow, sold the cow, land-lady sews proceeds in lining of his coat. On the way home, robbers [who had watched] took him and he scatters the money. They collect it and he, meanwhile, jumps on their horse.*)

"When they were gathering up the money that was strown,
I jumped on the horse and away now I rode."

(*Goes home. His father says,*)

"I think for a boy you've done quite right
And played on them a Yorkshire Bite."

L

Recorded in Charlestown, New Hampshire, from the memory of Orlon Merrill; learned in the logging woods.

H. H. F., *Collector*
August 26, 1931

Structure: A¹ A² B C (2,2,2,3); Rhythm D but divergent;
Contour: arc; Scale: Aeolian

t.c. D.

The Crafty Farmer

Tr. M. O.

The Crafty Farmer

Johnny and a thief met on a road. The thief demanded his gold.

> All amongst the tall grass
> He strewed it all about.
> Rattledy, right,
> Follow, dee, day.

While this fellow was picking it up, Johnny he jumped a-horseback

> And hurrah he rode.

He told his master he'd been robbed

> And out of the saddlebag
> And out of them told
> Five hundred pounds
> In silver and gold.

Master says:

> "You well sold my cow."

On January 10, 1932, Mr. Merrill remembered these lines which he sang to H. H. F.:

> "Deliver up your money
> Without any strife
> For in this lonesome valley
> I will take away your life."

M

As recalled by Mrs. Ellen M. Sullivan of Springfield, Vermont.

H. H. F., Collector
November 14, 1939

(There is a song: A man sends his boy to market to sell the cow; he is followed by robbers. He went to see an old woman who sewed the gold in his frock. Robbers watched; they then waited and watched for his return home. He scattered the pennies in the grass; then the robbers started to pick them up:)

> While they were gathering up the money
> That was scattered in the grass,
> Jack jumped in the saddle
> And he rode away the horse.

(The farmer wondered how his cow turned out to be a horse:)

> "How did my cow turn out to be a horse?"

N

John Taggart of Greenfield, Massachusetts, remembered this fragment in March, 1940, when on a visit to H. H. F. He gave no title.

H. H. F., Collector
March, 1940

(A farmer sent a boy to market to sell a cow. Foot pads followed and saw that he stowed his money in the torn lining of his coat sleeves. Then he stopped for a bite to eat.)

> There sat a highwayman a-sipping his wine
> And he says to himself, "Now that money shall be mine."

(When the boy reached a lonely place on the way home, he was held up by the highwayman.)

> From the lining of his coatsleeve, the money he tore out
> And in the long grass he strewed it about.

(The highwayman cursed, dismounted, and went to picking up the money out of the grass. While he was so engaged, the

boy quickly mounted the horse and dashed away. He ar-
rived at his master's door, described what had happened,
and they examined the saddle-bags.)

And two brace of pistols. The boy says, "I vow,
I think, my good master, I've well sold your cow."

(There is a refrain after each verse, running:)

> Luddelly dell, luddelly dell,
> Luddelly doo a die, a diddy um,
> A liddy, iddy dell,
> Lidelly doo a die a day.

O

As sung by Jonathan Moses of Orford, New Hampshire.
Learned from his father.

M. Olney, Collector
November 18, 1942

Structure: A B C (2,2,3); Rhythm C; Contour: arc; Scale:
Aeolian

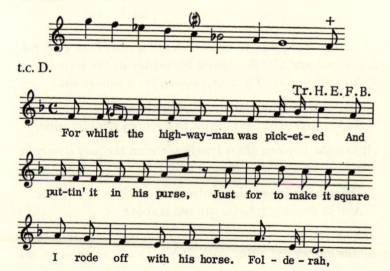

t.c. D.

did-dle-o-dow,   Fol - de-rah-rah,   fa - did-dle-o-day.

For whilst the highwayman was picketed
And puttin' it in his purse,
Just for to make it square
I rode off with his horse.
    Fol-de-rah, diddle-o-dow,
    Fol-de-rah-rah, fa-diddle-o-day.

The lady being young she saw John coming in.
She run to her kind master, so quicklie did explain.
His master coming out, he did curse and did swear,
"What the devil! Has my cow turned into a mare?"

   (*Repeat refrain after each stanza.*)

"For that's for the cow I sold," said John;
"Been robbed on the way by a highwayman bold
And whilst he was picketed and putting it in his purse,
Just for to make it square, I rode off with his horse."

Then out of the saddle-bags the money he pulled out,
A brace of bad pistols; says John, "I vow,
I think, my kind master, I've well sold your cow!"

The Coast of Barbary

(Laws K33, related to Child 285)

"George Aloe and the Sweepstake" (Child 285), which the jailer's daughter sings in *The Two Noble Kinsmen*, is extremely rare in America and is not found in the Flanders Collection at all. However, the common sea ballad "The Coast of Barbary" telling a similar story is known widely in the States and to some extent in England. This song traces back to a piece written for the British Navy by Charles Dibden (1745–1814). Dibden based his composition on "George Aloe and the Sweepstake" but retained little of his model beyond the plot outline and the "Barbary" refrain. In songs based on Dibden's original, the man–of–war defeats a pirate or privateer, although the merchantman, *George Aloe,* originally conquered a French naval vessel.

The Flanders texts follow the usual songster versions known in New England. Flanders A, very close to the A text in Phillips Barry's *British Ballads from Maine,* 413, is also like *The American Songster* (New York) version, as are the Flanders E and F fragments. Flanders B and C follow *The Forget-me-not Songster* (Turner and Fisher, Philadelphia) text, which in turn is like an old American broadside now in the Massachusetts Historical Society library and given as Barry D.

See Coffin, 152–3, for American bibliography to "George Aloe" and to the "Coast of Barbary." Laws, *ABBB,* 157–8, and Dean–Smith, 58, list the latter song.

The tunes for Child 285 are related, but not closely, with the exception of the Kneeland and Delano tunes. Tunes for this ballad are exceedingly rare in the standard American collections.

A

Recited by Maude Lyman Stevens of Newport, Rhode Island, who says, "This ballad was heard by Admiral Washburn Maynard of the United States Navy in Newport in 1862."

M. Olney, Collector

The High Barbaree

Oh, once there were two ships, and two ships there were of
    fame.
Blow high, blow low, 'cause slow sail-ed we.
Oh, one was the King of Prussia, and the other was Archie
    of Spain,
Cruising down along the coast of the High Barbaree.

"Aloft there, aloft there," our gallant commander cried.
Blow high, blow low, 'cause slow sail-ed we.
"Look ahead, look astern, look to windward and to lee,"
Cruising down along the coast of the High Barbaree.

"Oh, there's nothing ahead, and there's nothing astern."
Blow high, blow low, 'cause slow sail-ed we;
"But there's a lofty freight a-windward and another one on
    our lee,"
Cruising down along the coast of the High Barbaree.

"Oh, is she a man-of-war or is she a privateer?"
Blow high, blow low, for slow sail-ed we.
"She is not a man-of-war, nor is she a privateer,"
Cruising down along the coast of the High Barbaree.

"Now hail-ah, oh hail-ah," our gallant commander cried.
Blow high, blow low, so sail-ed we.
"Oh, I'm a saucy pirate as this night you soon shall see,"
Cruising down along the coast of the High Barbaree.

Then broadside, for broadside, this daring dog did pour,
Blow high, blow low, for slow sail-ed we,
Till the man at the helm shot the pirate's mast away,
Cruising down along the coast of the High Barbaree.

Then for mercy, for mercy, this daring dog did cry,
Blow high, blow low, for so sail-ed we.
"Oh, the mercy I will give you, I will sink you in the sea,"
Cruising down along the coast of the High Barbaree.

"Your ship shall be your coffin and your grave shall be the
    sea,"
Blow high, blow low, for slow sail-ed we.
"This your ship shall be your coffin and your grave shall
    shall be the sea,"
Cruising down along the coast of the High Barbaree.

B

*The words of this ballad were written down by Mrs. Bertha
J. Kneeland of Searsport, Maine, in 1914, from the singing
of her father-in-law, James Henry Kneeland, whose grandfather, Edward Kneeland, came to Cape Jellison from Boston about 1785.*

M. Olney, Collector
June 17, 1941

Structure: A B C D (2,2,2,2); Rhythm generally D; Contour:
arc; Scale: Aeolian

t.c. A.

Cruising Down on the Coast of Barbary

Tr. H. E. F. B.

Two ships, two ships, from Eng-land they came, Blow high, blow low, and so sail-ed we; One was the Prince of Lu-ther and the oth-er, Prince of Wales, Cruis-ing down on the coast of Bar-ba-ry.

Cruising Down on the Coast of Barbary

Two ships, two ships, from England they came,
Blow high, blow low, and so sail-ed we;
One was the Prince of Luther and the other, Prince of
    Wales,
Cruising down on the coast of Barbary.

Our boatswain up in our foretop did stand,
Blow high, blow low, and so sail-ed we;
"Look ahead, look astern, look to weather and to lee,"
Cruising down on the coast of Barbary.

"There is nothing ahead, there is nothing astern,"
Blow high, blow low, and so sail-ed we,
"But I see a ragged wind and a lofty ship at lee,"
Cruising down on the coast of Barbary.

"Ahoy! Ahoy!" our jolly captain cried,
Blow high, blow low, and so sail-ed we;

"Are you a man-of-war or a privateer?" said he,
Cruising down on the coast of Barbary.

"I am not a man-of-war, nor a privateer," said he,
Blow high, blow low, and so sail-ed we,
"But I am a jolly pirate, cruising for my fee,"
Cruising down on the coast of Barbary.

"If you're not a man-of-war nor a privateer," said he,
Blow high, blow low, and so sail-ed we,
"It is now to your guns, boys, and we'll show them pirate
    play,"
Cruising down on the coast of Barbary.

"A broadside! a broadside!" our jolly captain cried;
Blow high, blow low, and so sail-ed we;
At length the Prince of Luther cut the pirate's masts away,
Cruising down on the coast of Barbary.

. . . .
. . . .

We lashed them back to back, threw them all into the sea,
Cruising down on the coast of Barbary.

C

Sung by Mrs. Belle Richards of Colebrook, New Hampshire.
                                    M. Olney, Collector
                                    November 21, 1941

Structure: A B C (6,6,4); Rhythm B; Contour: arc; Scale:
hexatonic

t.c. E.

The Coast of Barbaree

Tr. M. O.

'Twas of two loft-y ves-sels came sail-ing o'er the sea;____ Blow high,____ blow low,____ for so sailed we. One____ was the Prince of Lu-ther and the oth-er, the Prince of Wales, As we sailed a-long the coast____ of Bar-ba-ree.

The Coast of Barbaree

'Twas of two lofty vessels came sailing o'er the sea;
Blow high, blow low, for so sailed we.
One was the Prince of Luther and the other, the Prince of
    Wales,
As we sailed along the coast of Barbaree.

"I'll speak her, I'll speak her," this gallant captain cries;
Blow high, blow low, for so sailed we.
"Are you a man-o'-war or a privateer?" cried he,
As we sailed along the coast of Barbaree.

"I am not a man-o'-war, nor a privateer," cried he;
Blow high, blow low, for so sailed we.
"But I am as jolly a pirate as ever sailed the sea,"
As we sailed along the coast of Barbaree.

"If you're not a man-o'-war or a privateer," cried he,
Blow high, blow low, for so sailed we;
"If you are a jolly pirate, I will sink you in the sea,"
As we sailed along the coast of Barbaree.

Then broadside to broadside his gallant ships did pay;
Blow high, blow low, for so sailed we;
And soon the Prince of Luther shot the pirate's mast away,
As we sailed along the coast of Barbaree.

.   .   .   .
.   .   .   .

The ship it was a scalpin[1] and his grave was in the sea,
As we sailed along the coast of Barbaree.

D

Sung by Mrs. Lena Bourne Fish of East Jaffrey, New Hampshire, as learned from an old man who was a sailor when she was a young girl.

M. Olney, Collector
July 16, 1942

Structure: A B C♭ D (4,4,4,4); Rhythm D; Contour: arc;
Scale: largely Aeolian

t.c. C.

[1] scalpin: "coffin" probably.

Along the Coast of High Barbary

Tr. H. E. F. B.

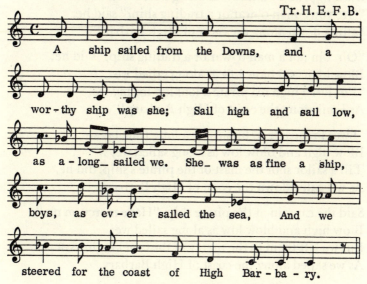

A ship sailed from the Downs, and a wor-thy ship was she; Sail high and sail low, as a-long sailed we. She was as fine a ship, boys, as ev-er sailed the sea, And we steered for the coast of High Bar-ba-ry.

Along the Coast of High Barbary

A ship sailed from the Downs, and a worthy ship was she;
Sail high and sail low, as along sailed we.
She was as fine a ship, boys, as ever sailed the sea,
And we steered for the coast of High Barbary.

"Aloft there, aloft," our bos'n cried, said he;
Blow high and blow low as along sailed we.
"Look ahead and look astern, look a-weather and look alee,
And look along the coast of High Barbary."

"There's nothing on the stern and there's naught upon the lee,"
Blow high and blow low as along sailed we.
"But there's a ship to windward a-sailing fast and free,
Sailing down along the coast of High Barbary."

"Oh, hail, there, oh, hail," our captain said, said he;
Blow high and blow low as along sailed we.
"Are you a man-o'-war or a trading ship?" said he,
Sailing down along the coast of High Barbary.

"Oh, I'm not a man-o'-war or a trading ship," said he;
Blow high and blow low as along sailed we.
"I'm just a high sea pirate a-looking for my fee
As I sail along the coast of High Barbary."

'Twas broadside to broadside a long time lay we;
Blow high and blow low as along sailed we,
Till a sailor shot the mast of the pirate's ship, did he,
As we sailed down the coast of High Barbary.

Said the captain of the pirate ship, "Have mercy on me";
Blow high and blow low as along sailed we;
But we left them to the mercy of the cruel raging sea
As we sailed along the coast of High Barbary.

E

Sung by Jack McNally of Stacyville, Maine.

M. Olney, Collector
August 26, 1942

Structure: A B C D (2,2,2,2); Rhythm C and D; Contour:
arc; Scale: Dorian

t.c. A.

Coast of New Barbaree

Tr. H. E. F. B.

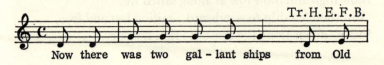

Now there was two gal-lant ships from Old

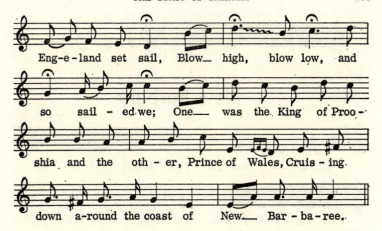

Eng-e-land set sail, Blow— high, blow low, and
so sail - ed we; One— was the King of Proo -
shia and the oth - er, Prince of Wales, Cruis - ing.
down a-round the coast of New— Bar - ba - ree.

Coast of New Barbaree

Now there was two gallant ships from Old Engeland set sail,
Blow high, blow low, and so sail-ed we;
One was the King of Prooshia and the other, Prince of Wales,
Cruising down around the coast of New Barbaree.

"Look to larboard, look to starboard, look to win'ward and
    to lee";
Blow high, blow low, and so sail-ed we;
"I see nothing in the larboard, I see nothing in the lee,
I see something in the starboard like the lofty ship at sea,"
Cruising down around the coast of New Barbaree.

F

*Recorded in Gassets, Vermont, from the singing of Wellman
J. Delano, learned in the Maine lumberlands at the age of
twelve. Printed in Vermont Folk-Songs & Ballads, 229.*

> *George Brown, Collector
> September 19, 1930*

Structure: A B C D (4,4,4,4); Rhythm D but dotted; Contour: arc; Scale: major, then Mixolydian

t.c. G.

New Barbary

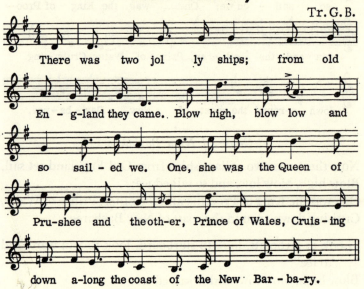

There was two jol ly ships; from old
En - g-land they came. Blow high, blow low and
so sail - ed we. One, she was the Queen of
Pru-shee and the oth-er, Prince of Wales, Cruis-ing
down a-long the coast of the New Bar - ba-ry.

New Barbary

There was two jolly ships; from old England they came.
Blow high, blow low and so sail-ed we.
One, she was the Queen of Pru-shee and the other, Prince of
    Wales,
Cruising down along the coast of the New Barbary.

"Oh, sailor, oh sailor," this jolly captain cried,
Blow high, blow low and so sail-ed we.

G

*Adam Morris, a restaurant keeper at Kingman, Maine, spoke
of his grandmother—a McPhail, who died at the age of 92—*

who had "Drempt a song—drempt she heard two sailors singing an old sea-song." Mr. Morris remembered a fragment of a song his mother sang to him. He sang it to the dictaphone set upon his lunch counter, to the great delight of a Passamaquoddy Indian.

H. H. F., Collector
July 11, 1940

New Barbary

"You are a saucy pirate, so you do say,"
Blow high, blow low, and so sail-ed we.
"Point out your Spanish guns and we'll show you British
    play,"
Cruising down along the coast of New Barbary.

Broadside to broadside these two ships they came;
Blow high, blow low, and so sail-ed we.
We shot the saucy pirate's three masts away,
Cruising down along the coast of New Barbary.

The Sweet Trinity or the Golden Vanity
(Child 286)

This ballad is immensely popular in America and not hard to find in Britain. It dates back to a broadside of the 1680's in which the deceitful captain is Sir Walter Raleigh. (See Flanders FF.) Since then it has taken many forms and may conclude in any number of ways. The Flanders texts give an excellent cross section of the plot variations found in this ballad. In A–T the boy drowns in the lowlands low. In U, he sinks the captain's ship as well as that of the enemy before he drowns. In V, he also sinks the captain's ship and there is only one survivor to tell the tale. In W, he sinks the captain's ship, ironically drowning the girl he loved with the crew. In X, he dies after being hauled on deck. In EE his ghost returns to treat the captain to a glass of beer before sinking the boat. In FF–JJ, the heroic lad is rewarded with a leave of absence, the daughter's hand, or gold and silver. Of these texts, A[1], with the stanzas on the phantom ship, and R, with the lines borrowed from "The Mermaid" (Child 289) are noteworthy. So are V, with its one survivor, like Melville's Ishmael; and FF, which preserves the name of Raleigh, if not the ending, from Child A. The vessel's name, originally *The Sweet Trinity,* varies greatly in America, becoming *The Golden Vanity, The Green Willow Tree, The Merry Golden Tree,* and so on. Its opponent, sunk by the cabin boy, was "a false galley" in the old broadside, but it is more likely a *Turkish* (or *Russian, Irish, French,* etc.) *Revelee* or *"Shavaree"* (sloop) in the States.

188

There is a certain preposterous quality to this song, and college students and music hall writers have exploited this fact in a series of parodies. See Coffin, 155, for references. Perhaps for the same reason, it has been extremely popular with sailors.

A long bibliography for "The Sweet Trinity" is easy to come by. See Coffin, 153–5 (American); Dean–Smith, 69; Belden, 97 (English); Greig and Keith, 228–9, and Ord, 450–1 (Scottish). Phillips Barry, *British Ballads from Maine,* 339–47, includes and discusses it. There is a song, once in a while confused with "The Sweet Trinity," called "The Lowlands Low." While it has a similar burden, it tells a very different story and goes back to an English stall ballad, "Young Edwin in the Lowlands Low" (Laws M 34), that was well known here and in Britain. See Laws, *ABBB,* 197–8; Belden, 127; and Dean–Smith, 118, for some references to it.

The tunes for Child 286 can be divided into six groups which, however, may turn out to be related at least to some extent. The groupings are as follows: (1) Davis, Edwards, Moses, Burditt, and possibly Pease; (2) George, Daniels, Houghton; (3) Henry, Blake, George, Barry; (4) Clarke, Cassidy, Richards, Dragon; (5) Ingalls; and (6) Fish and Percival. The Ingalls tune seems to be a version of the popular "Canada–I–O." In order to save repetition, the tune relationships for standard collections are given here. Only relatively close tunes have been selected from the large number available. In spite of their profusion, however, there is a lack of analogues for groups (2) and (6). For group (1), see Sharp 1, 282–285, 289 I; FCB 4, 120, 47 A, 121 A (I), 123 C (I); BES, 346; RO1, 195, 200 (D); BI, 160. For group (3), especially the Blake tune, see BES, 345 (distant). For group (4) see Sharp 1, 287, 288 G; GCM, 214; RO1, 200.

A^1

Mrs. Alice Sicily of North Calais, Vermont, recalled this song as sung by her grandfather, Elisha Slayton, "who used to sing it in the old-fashioned tune." He died when Mrs. Sicily, now (1933) 45, was 14 years old. Mrs. Sicily's father and grandfather were farmers.

H. H. F., *Collector*
July 29, 1933

Three Ships

There was a ship sailing on the sea
And the name of the ship was The Golden Willow Tree,
Sailing o'er the Lowlands low, down low,
Sailing o'er the Lowlands low.

(Repeat same refrain after each stanza except as indicated.)

The captain was a man of high degree
And he plied his trade upon the high sea.

He had a handsome wife and fair daughters three.
He sailed his ship for a far countree.

There was a ship sailing on the southern sea
And the name of the ship was The Turkey Shageree.

The captain of the ship was a man of low degree
And he preyed upon the ships that sailed the high seas.

The captain of the ship, a bad man was he.
He had neither wife, ne'er any familee.

(One of the captains was a pirate.)

He loaded the ship with provisions and with gold.
He had a rich cargo of silks in the hold.

He called to his sailors and he called to his men
And they all step-ped up to be at his command.

And he called to his wife and his fair daughters three
And they all stepped on board on The Golden Willow Tree.

He set his sails for a far countree
(*Cabin boy was bound to the captain*)

. . . .
". . . . . . what'll you give me
If I sink her in the Lowlands, *etc.*?"

"I will give you gold and I'll set you free
And the choice of my daughters your wedded wife shall be,
If you sink her, *etc.*"

"I care not for your daughters and I care not to be free
But ten thousand pounds of gold my price shall be
If I sink her, *etc.*"

Now, my kind friends, the truth it must be told.
He agreed to sink the ship for ten thousand pounds in gold,
To sink it, *etc.*

He had an instrument made for the use
And he bored nine holes and he bored 'em all at once
And he sank her, *etc.*

He bent upon his breast and out swam he;
He swam 'til he came to The Golden Willow Tree
And he sank her, *etc.*

He bent upon his back and back swam he,
He swam until he came to The Golden Willow Tree.

"O captain, O captain, take me on board
And be unto me as good as your word,
For I sunk her, *etc.*"

Three times 'round went the gallant ship
And three times 'round went she,
Then three times 'round went the gallant ship

'Til she came to the bottom of the sea
And she lies in the Lowlands low, down low,
And she lies in the Lowlands low.

"My dear cabin boy, I can't take you on board
And be unto you as good as my word
If you sunk her, *etc.*"

"If it wasn't for the love that I have for my friends,
I'd do unto you as I'd do unto them,
And I'd sink you, *etc.*"

(*More conversation, but he didn't stay afloat very long. Sailors mutineered*—)
And the men they all (*did something*) when they heard his
command.

They grabbed the captain up and they tossed him in the sea,
Saying, "Good bait for the fishes your old carcass shall be,"
And they threw him in the Lowlands, *etc.*

He bent upon his head and down went he,
And he went to the bottom of the sea.

A phanthom[1] ship sails on the sea;
Upon the decks there's the captain and the boy.

And they're sailing hand in hand; you can see them from the
land.
They're doomed to sail forever and forever more.

They're on that phanthom[1] ship;
They're doomed to sail forever and they cannot reach the
shore.

A^2

*This version received from Mrs. Alice Sicily of North Calais,
Vermont, which she originally gave in July, 1933. She*

---

[1] As pronounced.

thought there were some errors in her July, 1933, recollec-
tion of the song. Copied literatim et punctatim.

H. H. F., *Collector*
December 14, 1933

The Three Ships

There were three ships sailing on the northern sea.
One was a merchant ship of high degree
And they call this ship the Turkey Shagaree;
One was a pirate ship of low degree
And the name of the ship was the Golden Willow Tree.
There is a phantom ship that sails the high seas.

The captain was a merchant of high degree
And he plied his trade upon the high sea.
O, the captain of the ship, a good man was he
And he had a handsome wife and fair daughters three.

There was a ship sailing on the sea
And the name of this ship was the Golden Willow Tree,
Sailing o'er the lowlands, lie so low,
Sailing o'er the lowlands low.

He called to his sailors and he called to his men
And they all slipped up to be at his command
Saying, "O the lowlands, lie so low,"
Saying, "O the lowlands low."

They loaded the ship with provisions and with gold.
He had a handsome cargo of silks in the hold,
Sailing o'er the lowlands, etc.

He called to his wife and his daughters three
And they step-ped on board the Golden Willow Tree
Sailing o'er the lowlands, etc.

Then up stepped the Captain of the Golden Willow Tree
And he set sail for a far countree,
Saying, "O the lowlands, lie so low," etc.

There was a ship sailing on the southern sea
And the name of the ship was the Turkey Shageree,
Sailing, etc.

The captain was a pirate of low degree
And he preyed upon the ships that sailed the high seas, etc.

O, the captain of the ship, a bad man was he;
He had neither wife or any familee, etc.

There were three ships a-sailing on the northern sea
Before we came in sight of the Turkish Shaveree
And we sunk 'em in the lowlands, etc.

Up steps a cabin boy saying, "What shall you give me
If I go and sink that Turkish Shaveree?
O, I will sink 'em in the lowlands, so lonesome low,
I will sink 'em in the lowlands low."

"O, I will give you gold and I will give you prize.
My oldest daughter shall be your bride,
If you'll sink 'em in the lowlands, etc."

He took his instruments and out went he
'Til he came to the Turkish Shaveree
And he sank 'em in the lowlands, etc.

Some run with their coats, some with their caps
Trying to stop that salty water gap,
For he had sunk 'em, etc.

Then he took his instruments and back swam he
'Til he came to the Green Willow Tree,
For he had sunk 'em, etc.

"O Captain, O Captain, I come for my prize
For I have sunk that Turkish Shaveree;
I have sunk 'em in the lowlands, etc."

"I'll neither give you gold or will I give you prize
For I'll serve you as you served them.
You have sunk 'em in the lowlands, etc."

B¹

Sung by Asa Davis of Milton, Vermont. Learned from his father, Joel Davis, of Duxbury, Vermont.[1]

H. H. F., Collector
June 23, 1939
Retake by M. Olney

Structure: A B C¹ C² (2,2,2,2); Rhythm D but divergent; Contour: undulating; Scale: Dorian (the leading tone appears only once).

t.c. D.

The Green Willow Tree

Tr. M. O.

'Twas of a gal-lant ship of North A-mer-i-kee
That went by the name of The Green Wil-low Tree,
That was sail-ing in the Low-lands, lone-some low,
That was sail-ing in the Low-lands low.

[1] In another retake Mr. Davis omitted Stanzas 6, 11, and 12. Otherwise the singing was almost identical, word for word. See also B².

The Green Willow Tree

'Twas of a gallant ship of North Amerikee
That went by the name of The Green Willow Tree,
That was sailing in the Lowlands, lonesome low,
That was sailing in the Lowlands low.

They had not sailed days past two or three,
Before they espied a Turkish galilee
That lie anchored in the Lowlands, lonesome low,
That lay anchored in the Lowlands low.

Then up spoke the cabin boy saying, "What will you give me
If I will but sink that Turkish galilee
That lies anchored in the Lowlands, lonesome low,
That lies anchored in the Lowlands low?"

"Oh, I will give you gold and I will give you fee;
Likewise my eldest daughter, your wedded wife shall be,
If you sink them in the Lowlands, lonesome low,
If you sink them in the Lowlands low."

He turned upon his back and away swam he
Until he came to the Turkish galilee
That lie anchored in the Lowlands, lonesome low,
That lie anchored in the Lowlands low.

Oh, he had instruments all fit for the use,
He cut right in slashes and in went the juice,
Crying, "I'll sink you in the Lowlands, lonesome low,
I will sink you in the Lowlands low."

Oh, some with their hats and some with their vats
They came for to stop those watering gaps,
Crying, "We're sinking in the Lowland low,
We are sinking in the Lowlands low."

He turned upon his back and away swam he
Until he came to The Green Willow Tree

That was waiting in the Lowlands, lonesome low,
That was waiting in the Lowlands low.

"Oh, now, Mr. Captain, will you be as good as your word
And will you take me here on board
For I've sunk 'um in the Lowlands, lonesome low,
I have sunk 'um in the Lowlands low."

"Oh, no, I will not be as good as my word
Nor neither will take you here on board
But I'll sink you in the Lowlands, lonesome low,
I will sink you in the Lowlands low."

"If it wa'n't for the respects that I owe your men,
I would serve you as I've served them;
I would sink you in the Lowlands, lonesome low,
I would sink you in the Lowlands low."

He turned upon his back and down sank he,
Saying, "Fare ye well to The Green Willow Tree
For I'm sinking in the Lowlands low
I am sinking in the Lowlands low."

(spoken)

B²

Sung by Asa Davis of Milton, Vermont. See Text B¹.

M. Olney, Collector
(Retake)

The Green Willow Tree

It was of a gallant ship of North Amerikee
That went by the name of The Green Willow Tree
That was sailing in the Lowlands, lonesome low,
That was sailing in the Lowlands low.

They had not sailed days past two or three,
Before they espied a Turkish galilee

That lay anchored in the Lowlands, lonesome low,
That lay anchored in the Lowlands low.

Up spoke the cabin boy saying, "What will you give to me
If I will but sink that Turkish galilee
That lies anchored in the Lowlands, lonesome low,
That lies anchored in the Lowlands low?"

"Oh, I will give you gold and I will give you fee;
Likewise my oldest daughter, your wedded wife shall be,
If you sink them in the Lowlands, lonesome low,
If you sink them in the Lowlands low."

He turned upon his back and away swam he
Until he came to the Turkish galilee
That lie anchored in the Lowlands, lonesome low,
That lie anchored in the Lowlands low.

Then he had instruments all fit for the use,
He cut right in slashes and in went the juice,
Crying, "We are sinking in the Lowlands, lonesome low,
We are sinking in the Lowlands low."

He turned upon his back and away swam he
Until he came to The Green Willow Tree
That was waiting in the Lowlands, lonesome low,
That was waiting in the Lowlands low.

"Now, Mr. Captain, will you be as good as your word
And will you take me here on board?
For I've sunk 'um in the Lowlands, lonesome low,
I have sunk 'um in the Lowlands low."

"Oh, no, I will not be as good as my word
Nor neither will take you here on board,
But I'll sink you in the Lowlands, lonesome low,
I will sink you in the Lowlands low."

C

Recorded by H. H. F., July 29, 1931 in Springfield, Vermont, from the memory of Elwin Burditt who first heard this sung in his father's lumber mill in 1870, in Shrewsbury, Vermont.

George Brown, Collector
1930

Structure: A B C D (2,2,2,2); Rhythm D but divergent; Contour: undulating; Scale: hexatonic

t.c. F. Note the small range (major sixth).

Lowlands Low

Tr. M. O.

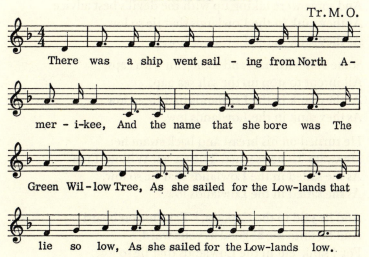

Lowlands Low

There was a ship went sailing from North Amerikee,
And the name that she bore was The Green Willow Tree,

As she sailed for the Lowlands that lie so low,
As she sailed for the Lowlands low.

She had sailed scarce three leagues, three,
Before she overtook The Turkish Revelee
As she sailed for the Lowlands that lie so low,
As she sailed for the Lowlands low.

"I'll give you gold and I'll give to you a fee
And I have an only daughter that I will marry unto thee,
If you'll sink 'em in the Lowlands that lie so low,
If you'll sink 'em in the Lowlands low."

Then he took an instrument made for that use
To make four and twenty holes, all in one push,
And he sank 'em in the Lowlands that lie so low
And he sank 'em in the Lowlands low.

Some were playing cards and some were playing dice
And some were taking up with the devil's best advice
As they sank in the Lowlands that lie so low,
As they sank in the Lowlands low.

Some run with hats and some run with caps,
All intent to stop up the salt sea gap,
As they sank in the Lowlands that lie so low,
As they sank in the Lowlands low.

He turned on his breast and back swam he;
He swam 'til he reached The Green Willow Tree
As she sailed in the Lowlands that lie so low,
As she sailed in the Lowlands low.

And he said to the Captain, "Take me on board
And be unto me as good as your word,
For I sank 'em in the Lowlands that lie so low,
For I sank 'em in the Lowlands low."

Then said the Captain, "I'll not take you on board
Nor be unto you as good as my word.

You can sink in the Lowlands that lie so low,
You can sink in the Lowlands low."

"Were it not for the love that I have for your men,
I would do unto you as I did unto them.
I would sink you in the Lowlands that lie so low,
I would sink you in the Lowlands low."

He turned on his breast and away swam he.
He swam straight away from The Green Willow Tree
And he sank in the Lowlands that lie so low
And he sank in the Lowlands low.

D

Copied from the manuscript in the scrapbook of Mrs. Altie Dean Sanders of Mt. Holly, Vermont (born 1860), as furnished by Mrs. Lloyd Wilkins of Rutland, Vermont.

H. H. F., Collector
May 4, 1932

Green Willow Tree

There was a ship a sailing in north america
The name of it was the green willow tree
As she sailed in the low lands that lies so low
As she sailed in the low lands low,

She had not sailed a league scarce three
Before she overtook the turkey shrevelee
As she sailed in the low lands that lie so low
As she sailed in the low lands low.

Then up steped the cabin boy saying what will you giv me
If I will go and sink the turkey shrevelee
If Ill sink her in the low lands that lie so low
If ill sink her in the low lands low

Oh I will give you gold and i will give you fee
Beside an only daughter ill marry unto thee

If you'l sink her in the low lands that lie so low
If you'l sink her in the low lands low

He turned upon his breast and out swam he
Untill he overtook the turkey srevelee
As she sailed in the low lands that lie so low
As she sailed in the low lands low

He having an instrument all fitted for the use
To make four and twenty holes all at one push
As she sailed in the low lands that lie so low
As she sailed in the low lands low,

Some wer playing cards and some wer playing dice
And they all wer taking up with the Devil's best advice
As he sank her in the low lands that lie so low
As he sank her in the low lands low,

Some ran with hats others ran with caps
All for to stop up the salt watter gaps
As she sank in the low lands that lie so low
As she sank in the low lands low.

He turned upon his breast and back swam he
Untill he over took the green willow tree,
As she sailed in the low lands that lie so low
As she sailed in the low lands low,

He ses unto the captain will you take me on board
And will you be to me as good as your word.
For ive sunk them in the low lands that lie so low
I have sunk them in the low lands low

Oh no ses the captain i'll not take you on board
Nor will i be to you as good as my word
You may go to the low lands that lie so low
You may go to the low lands low,

Wer it not for the love that i have for your men
I would do unto you as i've done unto them

I would sink you in the low lands that lie so low
I would sink you in the low lands low,

He turned upon his breast and out swam he
He bid fare well to the green willow tree
As she sailed in the low lands that lie so low
As she sailed in the low lands low,

E

*Elmer George of East Calais, Vermont, learned this song
some forty years ago from a lumberjack, Frank Layton, who
had "lived everywhere on the face of the globe; never had a
home in his life. He had a golden voice." Published in*
Country Songs of Vermont, *40.*[1]

H. H. F., Collector
Early 1930's

Structure: A^1 A^2 A^3 B C^{b1} C^{b2} (2,2,2,2,2,2); Rhythm D; Contour: undulating; Scale: Mixolydian

t.c. C.

The Golden Willow Tree

Tr. H. E. F. B.

There___ was   a___ ship   in   the

[1] In another singing of the song, Mr. George left out the next to last stanza and used the title "The Turkish Shagaree." In a third singing, in 1947, however, he included the stanza and again used the "The Golden Willow Tree" title.

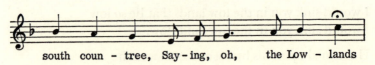

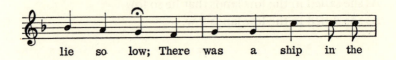

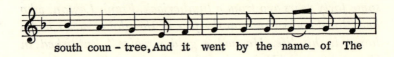

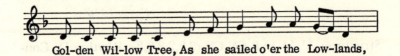

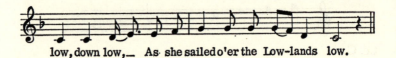

The Golden Willow Tree

There was a ship in the south countree,
Saying, oh, the Lowlands lie so low;
There was a ship in the south countree,
And it went by the name of The Golden Willow Tree,
As she sailed o'er the Lowlands, low, down low,
As she sailed o'er the Lowlands low.

There was another ship in the same countree,
Sailing o'er the Lowlands lie so low,
There was another ship in the same countree
And it went by the name of The Turkish Shageree,

And she sailed in the Lowlands, low, down low,
And she sailed in the Lowlands, low.

Oh, up speaks one little cabing boy,
Saying, oh, the Lowlands lie so low,
Oh, up speaks one little cabing boy,
Saying, "What would you give me if the ship I'll destroy,
If I'll sink her in the Lowlands, low, down low,
If I'll sink her in the Lowlands, low?"

"Oh, I'll give you gold and I'll give you fee,"
Saying, oh, the Lowlands lie so low,
"Oh, I'll give you gold, and I'll give you fee,
And my oldest daughter your wedding-bride shall be,
If you'll sink her in the Lowlands, low, down low,
If you'll sink her in the Lowlands, low."

He bent upon his breast and away swam he,
Saying, oh, the Lowlands lie so low;
He bent upon his breast and away swam he,
And he swam till he came to The Turkish Shageree,
As she sailed o'er the Lowlands, low, down low,
As she sailed o'er the Lowlands, low.

He had an instrument was fixed for the use,
Saying, oh, the Lowlands lie so low,
He had an instrument was fixed for the use
And he bored nine holes and he bored 'em all to once,
And he sank her in the Lowlands, low, down low,
And he sank her in the Lowlands, low.

Then he bent upon his back and back swam he,
Saying, oh, the Lowlands lie so low,
He bent upon his back and back swam he,
And he swam till he came to The Golden Willow Tree,
As she sailed o'er the Lowlands, low, down low,
As she sailed o'er the Lowlands, low.

"O capting, O capting, oh, take me on board,"
Saying, oh, the Lowlands lie so low,
"O capting, O capting, oh, take me on board
And be unto me as good as your word,
For I've sunk her in the Lowlands, low, down low,
For I've sunk her in the Lowlands, low."

"Oh, no, oh, no, I won't take you on board,"
Saying, oh the Lowlands lie so low,
"Oh, no, oh, no, I won't take you on board,"
Nor be unto you as good as my word,
If you've sunk her in the Lowlands, low, down low,
If you've sunk her in the Lowlands, low."

"If it wasn't for the love that I have for your men,"
Saying, oh, the Lowlands lie so low,
"If it wasn't for the love that I have for your men,
I would do unto you as I did unto them,
I would sink you in the Lowlands, low, down low,
I would sink you in the Lowlands, low."

He wrote a message and sent it to his friends,
Saying, oh, the Lowlands lie so low,
He wrote a message and sent it to his friends,
To let them know of his dreadful end,
And he sank in the Lowlands, low, down low,
And he sank in the Lowlands, low.

He bent upon his head and down swam he,
Saying, oh, the Lowlands lie so low,
He bent upon his head and down swam he,
And he swam till he came to the bottom of the sea,
And he lays in the Lowlands, low, down low,
And he lays in the Lowlands, low.

F^1

*Sung by Miss Emily Josephine Chism (eighty-five years old)
in Westford, Connecticut. Miss Chism said that her father's*

*cousin, Mrs. Royal Chapman, heard this sung by a stray
fellow working for the Curtisses, a family she was intimate
with.*

H. H. F., *Collector*
September 23, 1956

The Golden Willow Tree

There once was a captain who went out to sea,
And the name of his ship was The Golden Willow Tree,
And he sailed along the Lowlands, Lowlands,
He sailed along the Lowlands, low.

He had not been out more than two days or three
When he was overtaken by a Turkish gallee,
As they sailed along the Lowlands, Lowlands,
As they sailed along the Lowlands, low.

"O Captain," said the cabin boy, "what will you give to me
If I will swim across and sink the gallee?"
As they sailed along the Lowlands, Lowlands,
They sailed along the Lowlands, low.

"Oh, I will give you gold and to thee (?) quite a store
And also my daughter when you get on shore,
If you'll sink them in the Lowlands, Lowlands,
If you'll sink them in the Lowlands, low."

The boy took off his armour and jumped into the sea
And swam till he reached the Turkish gallee,
As he sailed along the Lowlands, Lowlands,
As he sailed along the Lowlands, low.

Then some were playing cards and some were playing dice.
He bored a hole into the ship and sunk her in a trice,
Away on the Lowlands, lowlands,
Away on the Lowlands, low.

"O Captain, O Captain, oh, take me on board
And be unto me as good as your word."

As they sailed along the Lowlands, Lowlands,
They sailed along the Lowlands, low.

"I will not," said the captain, "take you a-board
Nor neither will I be to you as good as my word,
Though you're sinking in the Lowlands, Lowlands,
Though you're sinking in the Lowlands, low."

The captain sailed away in this Golden Willow Tree
And left the little cabin boy a-sinking in the sea
Away on the Lowlands, Lowlands,
Away on the Lowlands, low.

F^2

*Sent to Mrs. Flanders by George Edwards of Burlington,
Vermont. "The Golden Vanity" was a ballad known and
used by his family for a very long time. Just how long it had
been handed down from generation to generation he did not
know. Copied literatim et punctatim.*

H. H. F., Collector
March 28, 1934

The Golden Vanity

Sir Walter Raleigh built a ship to sail the Netherland seas,
            Saying, oh, the lowlands, low,
Sir Walter Raleigh built a ship to sail the Netherland seas
And she went by the name of the Golden Vanity
            And they sunk her in the
            Lowlands, lowlands low,
            And they sunk her in the
            Lowlands, low.

The shipping in the lowlands they feared of her intent,
            Saying, oh, the lowlands, low,
The shipping in the lowlands they feared of her intent
For the mission was a secret one on which the ship was sent,
            And they sunk her in the

Lowlands, lowlands, low,
And they sunk her in the
Lowlands, low.

There was another ship from a neighboring country,
Saying, oh, the lowlands, low,
There was another ship from a neighboring country
And she sailed away in search of the Golden Vanity
And she sunk her in the
Lowlands, lowlands, low,
And she sunk her in the
Lowlands, low.

She sought the ship for many a day, and went from sea to sea,
Saying, oh, the lowlands, low,
She sought the ship for many a day, and went from sea to sea
Till at length she found her in a port, on the Zuyder Zee,
And she sunk her in the
Lowlands, lowlands, low,
And she sunk her in the
Lowlands, low.

Then up spake John, a brave young lad, he was the cabin boy,
Saying, oh, the lowlands, low,
Then up spake John, a brave young lad, he was the cabin boy
And he said to the captain "I can that ship destroy,"
"I can sink her in the
Lowlands, lowlands, low,
I can sink her in the
Lowlands, low.

G

*Sung by Paul Lorette of Manchester Center, Vermont, as
remembered from his brother, James Lorette. Published in*
Vermont Folk-Songs & Ballads, *230.*[1]

George Brown, Collector
September 23, 1930

[1] The published text differs ever so slightly from this one.

Lowlands Low

There were three ships a-sailing on the northern sea.
We hadn't sailed east no more than one or two days,
Before we came in sight of The Turkish Shaveree
As we sank 'em in the Lowlands, so lonesome low,
As we sank 'em in the Lowlands low.

Oh, up steps the cabin boy saying, "What shall you give me
If I go and sink that Turkish Shaveree?
Oh, I will sink 'em in the lowlands, the lonesome low,
I will sink 'em in the Lowlands low."

"Oh, I will give you gold and I will give you prize;
My oldest daughter shall be your bride
If you'll sink 'em in the Lowlands, the lonesome low,
If you'll sink 'em in the Lowlands low."

So he took his instruments and out went he
Till he came to The Turkish Shaveree,
And he sank 'em in the Lowlands, the lonesome low,
And he sank 'em in the Lowlands low.

Some run with their coats, and some with their caps
Trying to stop that salty water gap,
But he had sunk 'em in the Lowlands, so lonesome low,
He had sunk 'em in the Lowlands low.

Then he took his instruments and back swam he
Till he came to The Green Willow Tree,
For he had sunk 'em in the Lowlands, the lonesome low,
He had sunk 'em in the Lowlands low.

"O Captain, O Captain, I came for my prize
For I have sunk that Turkee Shaveree.

For I have sunk 'em in the Lowlands, the lonesome low,
I have sunk 'em in the Lowlands low."

"I will neither give you gold nor will I give you prize,
But I'll serve you as you've served them;
You have sunk 'em in the Lowlands, so lonesome low;
I will sink you in the Lowlands low."

H

*Sung to H. H. F. and Phillips Barry in Plainfield, Vermont,
by Mrs. Myra Daniels of East Calais, Vermont.*

H. H. F., Collector
October 22, 1935

Structure: A Bᵃ A C Dᶜ¹ Dᶜ² (2,2,2,2,2,2); Rhythm D; Contour: undulating; Scale: Mixolydian (the leading tone appears only once)

t.c. D.

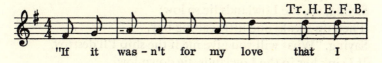

"If it was-n't for my love that I

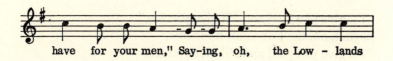

have for your men," Say-ing, oh, the Low - lands

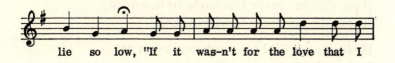

lie so low, "If it was-n't for the love that I

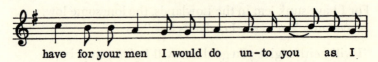

have   for your men   I would do   un-to you   as. I

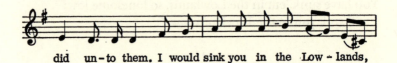

did   un-to them.   I would sink you   in the   Low - lands,

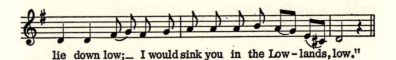

lie   down low;—   I would sink you   in the   Low - lands, low."

They had not sail-ed weeks but three,
Saying, oh, the Lowlands lie so low;
They had not sail-ed weeks but three
When they came in sight of the Turkish Shageree,
As she sailed the Lowlands, lie down low,
As she sailed the Lowlands, low.

Then up speaks one little cabing boy,
Saying, oh, the Lowlands lie so low;
Then up speaks one little cabing boy,
Saying, "What will you give me if the ship I'll destroy,
If I sink her in the Lowlands, lie down low,
If I sink her in the Lowlands, low?"

"I'll give you gold and I'll give you fee,"
Saying, oh, the Lowlands lie so low,
"I'll give you gold and I'll give you fee,
And my oldest daughter your wedded bride shall be
If you sink her in the Lowlands, lie down low,
If you sink her in the Lowlands, low."

He bent upon his breast and away swam he,
Saying, oh, the Lowlands lie so low;

He bent upon his breast and away swam he
And he swam till he came to that Turkish Shageree
As she sailed the Lowlands, lie down low,
As she sailed the Lowlands, low.

He had an instrument that's fixed for the use,
Saying, oh, the Lowlands lie so low;
He had an instrument that's fixed for the use
For to bore nine holes and he bored them all to once,
And he sank her in the Lowlands, low down low,
And he sank her in the Lowlands, low.

Then he bent upon his breast and back swam he,
Saying, oh, the Lowlands lie so low;
Then he bent upon his breast and back swam he
And he swam till he came to The Golden Willow Tree
As she sailed the Lowlands, lie down low,
As she sailed the Lowlands, low.

"O Captain, Captain, oh, take me on board,
Saying, oh, the Lowlands lie so low;
"O Captain, Captain, oh, take me on board
And be unto me as good as your word
For I've sunk her in the Lowlands, lie down low,
For I've sunk her in the Lowlands, low."

"Oh, no, oh, no, I can't take you on board,"
Saying, oh, the Lowlands lie so low;
"Oh, no, oh, no, I can't take you on board
Nor be unto you as good as my word
If you've sunk her in the Lowlands, lie down low,
If you've sunk her in the Lowlands, low."

"If it wasn't for my love that I have for your men,"
Saying, oh, the Lowlands lie so low,
"If it wasn't for the love that I have for your men
I would do unto you as I did unto them.

I would sink you in the Lowlands, lie down low;
I would sink you in the Lowlands, low."

I

Sung by Mrs. Christina Henry of Providence, Rhode Island.
Mrs. Henry was born in Scotland and lived there until she
became a young lady. She emphasized the fact that she was
quite small when she learned this ballad and that she had
never heard it given a title.

M. Olney, Collector
October 20, 1946

Structure: A¹ B A² C (2,2,2,2); Rhythm D; Contour: undulating; Scale: major

t.c. B flat.

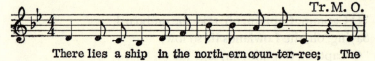

There lies a ship in the north-ern coun-ter-ree; The

name of · that ship is The . Gold-en Vic-to-ree.   The

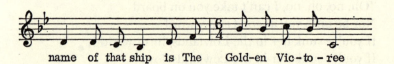

name of that ship is The   Gold-en Vic-to-ree

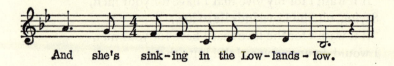

And   she's   sink-ing in the Low-lands-low.

There lies a ship in the northern coun-ter-ree;
The name of that ship is The Golden Victoree.
The name of that ship is The Golden Victoree
And she's sinking in the Lowlands-low.

Up spoke the Captain, and up spoke he,
"Is there anyone on board that will sink that ship for me?
Is there anyone on board that will sink that ship for me,
That will sink her in the Lowlands-low?"

Up spoke the cabin boy, and up spoke he,
"O Master, dear Master, what will you give to me?
O Master, dear Master, what will you give to me
If I sink her in the Lowlands-low?"

"I will give you silver, and I will give you gold,
The hand of my young daughter if you return bold;
The hand of my young daughter if you return bold,
If you sink her in the Lowlands-low!"

Away swam the cabin boy, away swam he,
With a dagger in his right hand to bear him company,
With a dagger in his right hand to bear him company,
And to sink her in the Lowlands-low.

Some were playing dominoes, and some were playing at cards.
The water rushing in gave them all a great surprise;
The water rushing in gave them all a great surprise.
They were sinking in the Lowlands-low.

Back came the cabin boy, and back came he.
"O Master, dear Master, do come and let me in.
O, Master, dear Master, do come and let me in,
For I've sunk her in the Lowlands-low!"

J

From Miss M. E. Beane, Irasburg, Vermont.

Phillips Barry, Collector

The Cabin Boy

There was a ship in the Northern Countrie,
All in the Lowland low,
The name of the ship was the Gold China Tree,
All in the Lowland low, low, low.
Sailing the Lowland, low, low, low,
Sailing the Lowland low.

She had not sailed past leagues two or three,
All in the Lowland low,
She had not sailed past leagues two or three
Before she espied a French galilee.

The first that spoke was the ship captain's man,
All in the Lowland low,
Saying, "Master, O Master, we're all undone,
All in the Lowland low, low, low!"

Next spoke up was the little cabin boy,
All in the Lowland low,
Saying, "Master, O Master, what will you give to me,
If I will sink the French galilee?"

"Oh, I will give you gold, and I will give you fee,
All in the Lowland low,
And my eldest daughter your bride shall be,
All in the Lowland low, low, low,"

He smote upon his breast, and away swung he,
All in the Lowland low,
He smote upon his breast, and away swung he,
And he swung till he came to the French galilee.

Then he espied a little augur that came from a nun,
All in the Lowland low,
Then he espied a little augur that came from a nun,
And bored holes with it, twenty and one.

Some threw their hats, and some threw their caps,
All in the Lowland low,
Saying, "For the Lord's sake, stop up the salt water gaps!
All in the Lowland low, low, low!"

K

*Sung by Mrs. Harriet Gott Murphy of Rumford Center,
Maine.*

M. Olney, Collector
September 12, 1942

Lowlands Low

My father owns a ship in the northern country;
She goes by the name of The Golden Vanity.
I fear she will be taken all by some Spanish crew,
As she sails along the Lowlands, along the Lowlands,
As she sails along the Lowlands low.

The first one that spoke up was a saucy cabin boy:
"Say, what will you give me if I will her destroy?"
"I'll give you gold and silver, my daughter fair and gay
If you'll sink her in the Lowlands, in the Lowlands,
If you'll sink her in the Lowlands low."

The boy he bent his breast and then he plunged in.
The boy he bent his breast and then began to swim.
He swam alongside of this large Spanish ship,
And he sank her in the Lowlands, in the Lowlands,
And he sank her in the Lowlands low.

Oh, some were playing cards and some were shaking dice
And some were in their hammocks a-sleeping very nice.
He bored two holes in her broadside and let the water in,
And he sank her in the Lowlands, in the Lowlands,
And he sank her in the Lowlands low.

The boy he swam back unto the starboard side,
And being quite exhausted, so bitterly he cried,

"Oh, messmates, take me in, for I'm going with the tide,
And I'm sinking in the Lowlands, in the Lowlands,
And I'm sinking in the Lowlands low."

"I will not take you in," our captain then replied,
"I will not give you gold nor my daughter for your bride.
I'll shoot you, I'll stab you, and send you with the tide,
And I'll sink you in the Lowlands, in the Lowlands,
And I'll sink you in the Lowlands low."

The boy, he then swam on unto the larboard side,
And being quite exhausted, so bitterly he cried,
"Oh, messmates, take me in, for I'm going with the tide,
And I'm sinking in the Lowlands, in the Lowlands,
And I'm sinking in the Lowlands low."

L

Mrs. Frederick Waters of Brattleboro, Vermont, remembered these stanzas from "The Virginal Three" from a sailor "named Hugh" singing to her mother, Mrs. Emma Robinson Titus of Burlington, Vermont. Mrs. Titus had learned them when a child of five, living in Barton, Vermont.

H. H. F., Collector
July 12, 1931

The Virginal Three

The captain he ordered his ship to sea,
Sailing in lowlands low.
The captain he ordered his ship to sea
And the name of it was The Virginal Three,
Sailing in the Lowlands, low, low, low,
Sailing in the Lowlands low.

(*Follow pattern of first stanza for all stanzas.*)

We had sailed but a night or two
When a Turkish galley hove up in view.

(Captain asked who will go and destroy it.)

Then speaks up this little cabin boy,
"Oh, what will you give me if the ship I'll destroy?"

"Oh, it's I'll give you gold and I'll give you fee
And when we get home, to my daughter married be."

(Boy takes tools and "He stuck three holes in one.")

He folded his arms across his breast
And away he swam to the captain and the rest.

(He gets there and the captain refuses to take him on board.)

"If it were not for the honor of your men . . ."

(Cabin boy says he'd take his tools and serve him the same.)

"I'd serve you the same."

(Mr. Bigelow, 13 Green Street, also knew this song and thought in the full version of this ballad the cabin boy was saved in some strange way and got home and married the captain's daughter.)

M

As sung by Jonathan Moses of Orford, New Hampshire.[1]

> Alan Lomax and H. H. F., Collectors
> Retake by M. Olney
> August 23, 1951

Structure: A B C D E[1] E[2] (2,2,2,2,2,2); Rhythm D; Contour: arc; Scale: Dorian (G sharp is only a neighbor tone between A's)

---

[1] Mr. Moses says, "There is much more to this one but it is all I can remember." In September, 1939, when he first sang it he could recall only the first two stanzas printed here.

t.c. D.

The Lowlands Low

Tr. M. O.

"O Cap - tain, O Cap - tain, oh, take me on board," Cry-ing oh, the Low - lands low. "O Cap - tain, O Cap-tain, oh, take me on board And be un - to me as good as your word, For I've sank them in the Low-lands, Low-lands so

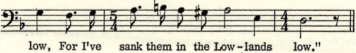

low, For I've sank them in the Low - lands low."

The Lowlands Low

"O Captain, O Captain, oh, take me on board,"
    Crying, oh, the Lowlands low.
"O Captain, O Captain, oh, take me on board
And be unto me as good as your word,
For I've sank them in the Lowlands, Lowlands so low,
For I've sank them in the Lowlands low."

"Oh, no!" said the captain, "I shan't take you on board."
    Crying, oh, the Lowlands low.
"Oh, no!" said the captain, "I shan't take you on board
Nor neither shall I be as good as my word,
For you've sank them in the Lowlands, Lowlands so low,
For you've sank them in the Lowlands low."

"O Captain, O Captain, oh, take me on board,"
    Crying, oh, the Lowlands low.
"O Captain, O Captain, oh, take me on board
For I'll do unto you as I did unto them,
For I sank you in the Lowlands, Lowlands so low,
For I sank you in the Lowlands low."

N

*Fragment recalled when John A. Taggart sang to H. H. F.
in Greenfield, Mass.*

H. H. F., *Collector*
October 1, 1939

Then he smote on his breast and he swam,
    Sailing in the Lowland, low,
Until unto Captain Ward's ship he did come,
    Sailing in the Lowland low.

(*It was a pirate ship which he wanted to destroy.*)

He put in his auger and gave it a bounce,
    Sailing in the Lowland, low,

And into her bottom he bored nine holes at once,
Sailing in the Lowland low.

(*He peeked through the holes and he saw—*)

Some were at cards, and some were at dice,
Sailing in the Lowland, low,
And some were taking the devil's advice,
Sailing in the Lowland low.

O

Printed in JAF, XVIII, 127. "Taken down by me, October 2, 1904, from the singing of J. G. M., Newbury, Vt." (A note from Mr. Barry to H. H. F. indicates that the singer was Mr. J. G. Marcy.)

Phillips Barry, Collector
October 2, 1904

The Golden Vanity

Once there was a ship in the Northern Counteree,
The title she went under was the Golden Vanity,
Supposed to have been taken by a Turkish canoe,
And sunken in the Lowlands low,
Lowlands, Lowlands low,
And sunken in the Lowlands low.

The first on the deck was the little Cabin Boy,
Saying, "Master, what'll you give me, if the ship I will destroy?"
"My gold I will give you, my daughter for a bride,
If you'll sink her in the Lowlands low!"

. . . .

. . . .

. . . bored holes three times three,
And sunk her in the Lowlands low.

P

As sung by Mrs. Mabel Pease of Orford, New Hampshire.

M. Olney, Collector
November 19, 1942

Structure: A¹ B¹ A² B² C D (2,2,2,2,2,2); Rhythm D but divergent; Contour: undulating and ascending; Scale: major

t.c. B flat.

Louisiana Lowlands Low

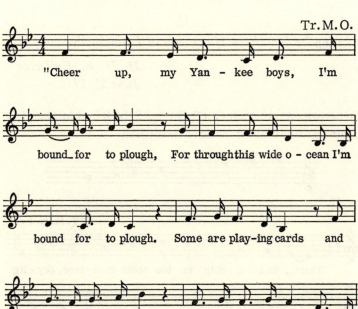

Tr. M. O.

"Cheer up, my Yan-kee boys, I'm bound for to plough, For through this wide o-cean I'm bound for to plough. Some are play-ing cards and some are play-ing dice, Daz-zled in the wa-ter and

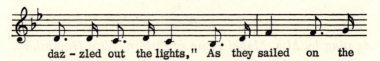

Louisiana Lowlands Low

"Cheer up, my Yankee boys, I'm bound for to plough
For through this wide ocean I'm bound for to plough.
Some are playing cards and some are playing dice,
Dazzled in the water and dazzled out the lights,"
As they sailed on the lowlands, lowlands,
Louisiana lowlands low.

Q

As sung by Mrs. Fred Houghton of Lyndon, Vermont.

H. H. F., *Collector*
June 25, 1942

Structure: A¹ A² A¹ B C¹ C² (2,2,2,2,2,2); Rhythm C and D;
Contour: undulating; Scale: Mixolydian

t.c. C.

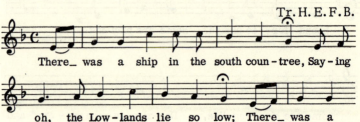

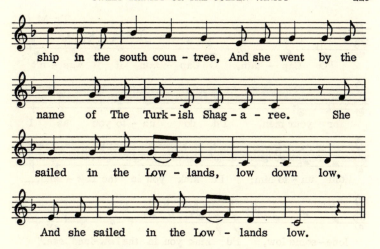

ship in the south coun - tree, And she went by the
name of The Turk - ish Shag - a - ree. She
sailed in the Low - lands, low down low,
And she sailed in the Low - lands low.

There was a ship in the south countree,
Saying, oh, the Lowlands lie so low;
There was a ship in the south countree,
And she went by the name of The Turkish Shagaree.
She sailed in the Lowlands, low down low,
And she sailed in the Lowlands low.

R

Recorded from the singing of Mrs. Naomi Ingalls of Windsor, Vermont, as learned from her father-in-law, Mr. Myron Ingalls of Windham, Vermont.

H. H. F., *Collector*

Structure: A B¹ B² C (2,2,2,2); Rhythm D; Contour: arc; Scale: hexachordal

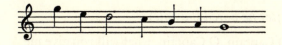

t.c. C.

Tr. M. O.

"O Cap - tain, O Cap - tain, if it was - n't
for your men, I'd do un - to you as I
did un - to him; I'd sink you in the Low - land,—
lone - some low, I'd sink you in the Low-land sea."

"O Captain, O Captain, if it wasn't for your men,
I'd do unto you as I did unto him;
I'd sink you in the Lowland, lonesome low,
I'd sink you in the Lowland sea."

So three times 'round went that gallant ship
And three times 'round sailed she
And three times 'round went the gallant ship
And she sank to the depths of the sea.

S

Fragment known to Mrs. Norah Thurston of Woodbury, Vermont.

H. H. F., *Collector*

The Green Willow Tree

She sunk in the lowlands.

(*After he bored the hole*)

"O Captain, O Captain, what will you give me
To sink that ship, The Green Willow Tree?"

"I'll give you gold, I'll give you fee,
And my only daughter a wife for to be,
If you'll sink that ship, The Green Willow Tree,
If you sink her in the lowlands low."

T

Sent to H. H. F. from Amy Perkins of Rutland, Vermont.

H. H. F., Collector
November, 1931

Lowlands

(My mother says that her mother, Eliza [Craigue] Fisher, used to sing some of a song to which this was the chorus or an ending for the verses, seemingly an old pirate or privateer song.)

"We'll plant them in the lowlands,
None, none so low.
We'll plant them in the lowlands, low."

U

Recorded in Jamaica, Vermont from the singing of Mr. Fred Ballard, as learned from his mother, Mrs. Minerva Hathaway Ballard, who came to Vermont when she was one year old. Mrs. Ballard learned these songs from her mother and uncle; her father was a sea captain from Providence, Rhode Island, who was lost at sea soon after the birth of his daughter.

George Brown, Collector
August 27, 1930

The Green Willow Tree

There once was a ship in the north country.
It went by the name of The Green Willow Tree.
And he plowed the low lands that lie so low,
And he plowed the low lands low.

There was another ship in the same country
And went by the name of The Turkee Suguree,
And they plowed the low lands that lie so low,
And they plowed the low lands low.

"I'll give you gold, or I'll give fee,
Besides my only daughter, I'll marry unto thee,
If you'll sink 'em in the low lands that lie so low,
If you'll sink 'em in the low lands low."

He had an instrument all fitted for his use
To bore four and twenty holes all at a push
To sink 'em in the low lands that lie so low,
To sink 'em in the low lands low.

The boy sinks the Turkee Suguree *and upon being refused
to be allowed to board his own ship he sinks her also. Then
he plunges into the deep and drowns.*

V

*Sent by Mrs. Lena Bourne Fish of East Jaffrey, New Hamp-
shire, whose father, Stratton Bourne, was born in northern
Vermon. Copied literatim et punctatim.*

H. H. F., Collector
1940[1]

Structure: A B C D E F♭ (2,2,2,2,2,2); Rhythm D; Contour:
undulating; Scale: major

t.c. D.

---

[1] On May 9, 1940, Miss Olney recorded this song from Mrs. Fish in almost
identical form, as did Mrs. Flanders on November 6, 1940, and on January
5, 1943. (See tune.)

The Weeping Willow Tree

Tr. H. E. F. B.

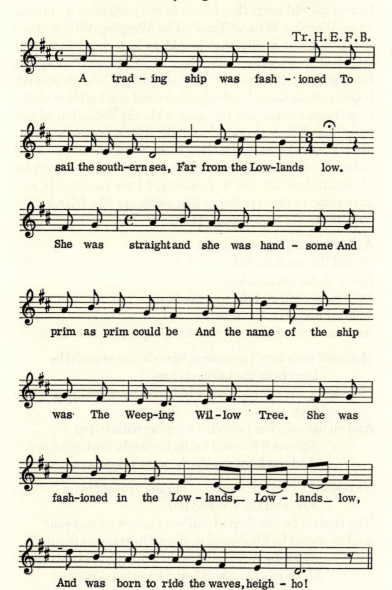

A trad-ing ship was fash-ioned To
sail the south-ern sea, Far from the Low-lands low.
She was straight and she was hand-some And
prim as prim could be And the name of the ship
was The Weep-ing Wil-low Tree. She was
fash-ioned in the Low-lands,— Low-lands— low,
And was born to ride the waves, heigh-ho!

The Weeping Willow Tree

One of the old songs that I have in my possession is entitled
"The Weeping Willow Tree." The Weeping Willow Tree
is the name of a ship that is said to have been built and
launched in Virginia in the days of Sir Walter Raleigh. It
is a tale of the lowlands of Virginia and Sir Walter Raleigh
is said to have named and superintended the building of the
ship. I have never put the song with any collection of old
songs that I have arranged as I thought it was so old that
no one would care for it. But when I see the collectors of
old songs have listed it as a rare old song and that few copies
of the original are now in existence, I have recopied it, and
have come to the conclusion that songs are like friends they
have to be old to be really good.

A Trading ship was fashioned
To sail the southern sea
Down in the lowland low
She was straight and she was handsome
And prim as prim could be
And the name of the ship was the Weeping Willow Tree

Her crew were hardy seamen as brave as brave could be
          Boys from the lowlands low,
Her decks were broad and wide, and were white as white
          could be
And on her sails was printed a weeping willow tree
          She was fashioned in the lowlands, lowlands low
          And was born to ride the wave heigh ho,

This worthy ship was chosen to sail the Spanish main
          Far from the lowland low
The captain he was shrewd and was also proud and vain
And he hoped by his shrewd dealing a fortune for to gain
          With the shipt built in the lowland, lowlands low
          That was born to ride the wave heigh ho

Now as this ship was sailing down on the southern sea
      Far from the lowland low
They met a Spanish ship called the Royal Castilee,
And they jeered at the crew of The Weeping Willow Tree,
That was faishn in the lowland, lowland low
      And was built to ride the wave hey ho.

The Captain called his cabin boy as he had done before
      A lad from the lowlands low
And he said boy you can swim and your stroke is swift and
      sure
So the saucy Spanish ship it shall never reach the shore
For we'll sink them in the ocean low, low low
      We will sink them in the ocean low.

So take in hand an auger and swim out to the side
      For we're from the lowlands low,
And then you bore a hole that shall be both deep and wide
For I am bound to humble the Spanish Sailor's pride
      And we'll sink them in the ocean low, low, low,
      We will sink them in the ocean low

So this was the end of the Royal Castilee
      She Sank in the ocean low
Her lofty sails so wide and her haughty air so free
Both were buried in the depths of the raging southern sea
      For they sank her in the ocean low, low, low
      They sank her in the ocean low

The cabin boy exclaimed sir, I now demand my fee
      You knave from the lowlands low
So five hundred lb in gold you now must give to me
And I also am first mate of the Weeping Willow Tree
      For I sank them in the ocean low, low, low
      I sank them in the ocean low

You'll get no gold from me lad for causing the wreck
      You thief from the low lands low

So he took the cabin boy the nape of the neck
And he flung him in the sea from the Weeping Willow's
    deck
That was fashioned in lowland, lowland low
    And was bui(l)t to ride the waves hey ho

But he still carried his auger as he had done before
    The lad from the lowland low
His heart was filled with vengeance his aim was swift and
    sure
So instead of boring one hole, he bored twenty-four
In the ship built lowlands, lowlands low
That was born to ride the wave hey ho

The worthy trading ship was 200 leagues from shore
    Far from the lowlands low
So the Captain and the crew they never reached the shore
And the wild seemed to say fare thee well for evermore
    To the ship built in the lowland, lowlands low
    That was born to ride the waves hey ho

But one brave hardy sailor escaped the raging sea
    A lad from the lowlands low
He was picked up by a ship so it has been told to me
And so he told the fate of the Weeping Willow Tree
    That was fashioned in the lowland, lowlands low
    And was bui(l)t to ride the wave hey ho

W

*Sung by Mrs. Mary Fitzgerald at the Perryville Grange,
Tuckertown, Rhode Island. Mrs. Fitzgerald tells the story
as follows: "It seems the Captain's daughter fell in love with
one of the seamen. The Captain told him he could have the
girl for his bride if he would swim out into the river or
pond and scuttle an enemy boat. In the meantime, he had
let his daughter go on board. When the fellow swims out*

to the boat, he bores the hole and scuttles it with the daughter on board."

H. H. F., *Collector*
November 21, 1944

Lowlands Low

My money you can't have,
Nor my daughter for your bride,
For you sunk them in the Lowlands low.

X

Sent by Albert R. Clarke, R. F. D., Perryville, Rhode Island,
February 12, 1945 and later recorded, April 5, 1945.[1]

H. H. F., *Collector*
February 12, 1945

Structure: A B A C D (2,2,2,2,2); Rhythm D but divergent;
Contour: undulating; Scale: major

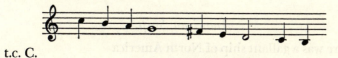

t.c. C.

American Ship

Tr. H. E. F. B.

There was   a gal – lant ship   of North   A–mer-

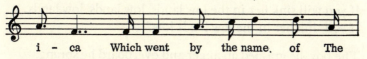

i – ca   Which went   by   the name.   of   The

[1] When Mr. Clarke was recorded, he made slight changes in some of the words; in lines 3 and 4, for example, he used "sanken" instead of "sunken." However, none of the changes were of any significance.

Gold - en Van - i - ty.   She was li - able to   be

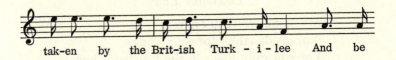

tak-en   by   the Brit-ish   Turk - i - lee   And   be

sank - en in   the low - lands,   low - lands, low - lands,

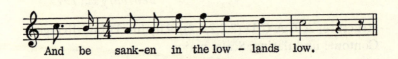

And   be   sank-en   in   the low - lands low.

American Ship

There was a gallant ship of North America
Which went by the name of "The Golden Vanity."
She was liable to be taken by the British Turkilee
And be sunken in the low lands, low lands, low lands,
And be sunken in the low lands low.

The first that came on deck was a little cabin boy,
Cried, "Captain, what will you give me if that ship I will
    destroy?"
"Gold I will give you, and my daughter for your bride,
If you will sink her in the low lands, low lands, low lands,
If you sink her in the low lands low."

The boy, he grasped an auger and overboard he sprang.
The boy, he bent his breast and out to sea he swam.
He swam to the side of the British Turkilee,

For to sink her in the low lands, low lands, low lands,
For to sink her in the low lands low.

Three holes he bored once; three holes he bored twice,
While some were playing cards and others shaking dice.
While some were playing cards, the waters they gushed in,
And he sank her in the low lands, low lands, low lands,
And he sank her in the low lands low.

The boy he bent his breast and back again he swam.
He swam to the side of "The Golden Vanity,"
Cried, "Captain, pick me up. I'm going with the tide;
I'm sinking in the low lands, low lands, low lands,
I'm sinking in the low lands low."

"For to pick you up, Oh, that I never will!
I'll shoot you; I'll kill you; I'll do it with a will.
Gold I'll never give you, nor my daughter for your bride,
But I'll bury you in the low lands, low lands, low lands,
I'll bury you in the low lands low.

The boy he bent his breast. On t'other side he swam.
He swam to the side of "The Golden Vanity,"
Cried, "Shipmates, pick me up. I'm going with the tide.
I'm a-sinking in the low lands, low lands, low lands,
I'm sinking in the low lands low."

The shipmates picked him up. 'Twas on the deck he died.
They wrapped him in his hammock, for it was long and
    wide
They wrapped him in his hammock and shoved him o'er the
    side,
And they buried him in the low lands, low lands, low lands,
And they buried him in the low lands low.

Y

Sung by Mrs. Alice Cassidy of East Matunuck, Rhode Island.

H. H. F., Collector
April 5, 1946

Structure: A B C D E (2,2,2,2,2); Rhythm D but divergent;
Contour: undulating; Scale: major

t.c. C.

Lowlands Low

Tr. H. E. F. B.

Lowlands Low

There was a gallant ship in North America;
It went by the name of The Golden Vanity.
It was liable to be taken by a British Turkilee
And be sunken in the Lowlands, Lowlands,
And be sunken in the Lowlands low.

The first on the deck was a little cabin boy,
Said: "Captain, what will you give me if I will that ship
    destroy?"
"Gold I will give you and my daughter for your bride,
If you'll sink her in the Lowlands, Lowlands,
If you'll sink her in the Lowlands low."

The boy he bent his breast and he swam with the tide;
He swam till he came to the Turkish side.
Three holes he bored once, three holes he bored twice,
For some were playing cards and others were shaking dice.
For some were playing cards and the waters they poured in
For she was sinking in the Lowlands, Lowlands,
For she was sinking in the Lowlands low.

The boy he bent his breast and he swam against the tide;
He swam till he came to The Golden Vanity's side,
Saying, "Captain, pick me up for I'm going with the tide.
I am sinking in the Lowlands, Lowlands,
I am sinking in the Lowlands low."

"Gold I'll not give you nor my daughter for your bride,
But I'll sink you in the Lowlands, Lowlands,
For I'll sink you in the Lowlands low."

The boy he bent his breast and he swam to the other side,
Saying, "Shipmates, pick me up for I'm going with the tide."
The shipmates picked him up and 'twas on the ship he died.
They sewed him in his hammock, which was both long and
    wide.

They sewed him in his hammock; it was both long and wide,
And they sank him in the Lowlands, Lowlands,
And they sank him in the Lowlands low.

Z

Sung by Mrs. Belle Richards of Colebrook, New Hampshire.

M. Olney, Collector

November 20, 1941

Structure: A B C D E (2,2,2,2,2); Rhythm D but divergent;
Contour: undulating; Scale: major

t.c. G.

The Golden Vanity

Tr. M. O.

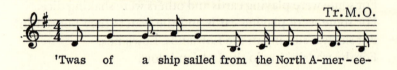

'Twas of   a ship sailed from the North A-mer-ee-

kay   And   she went   by   the name   of   The

Gold - en Van - i - ty   And   she feared she would be

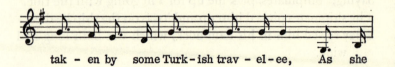

tak - en by   some Turk-ish trav - el-ee,   As   she

lay a-long the Low - lands, Low - lands,

As she lay a-long the Low - lands_ low.

The Golden Vanity

'Twas of a ship sailed from the North Amereekay
And she went by the name of The Golden Vanity
And she feared she would be taken by some Turkish
    travelee,
As she lay along the Lowlands, Lowlands,
As she lay along the Lowlands low.

The first that came on deck was a little cabin boy,
Saying, "Captain, what'll you give to me that ship for to
    destroy?"
"I will give you gold and silver and my daughter when on
    shore
If you'll sink her in the Lowlands, Lowlands,
If you'll sink her in the Lowlands low."

Oh, then he grasped an auger and overboard sprang he;
He smote upon his breast as he swam along the sea
And he swam till he came to the Turkish travelee,
As she lay in the Lowlands, Lowlands,
As she lay in the Lowlands low.

Oh, some were playing cards and some were shaking dice,
And some were in the cabin a-sleeping with their wives,
And he bored her good ship's bottom and he sank her in
    the tide,
As she lay along the Lowlands, Lowlands,
As she lay along the Lowlands low.

Oh, then he swam back to The Golden Vanity.
"Take me up, take me up, for I'm sinking in the sea.
Take me up, take me up, for I'm sinking in the tide,"
As they lay along the Lowlands, Lowlands,
As they lay along the Lowlands low.

"Take you up, take you up, no, that never can be.
I'll sink you, I'll drown you, in the bottom of the sea.
If you bored her good ship's bottom and you sank her in
    the tide,
You may sink in the Lowlands, Lowlands,
You may sink in the Lowlands low."

"O Captain, brave Captain, if it wasn't for your men,
I would do unto you as I've done unto them.
I would bore your good ship's bottom and I'd sink you in
    the tide,
As you lay along the Lowlands, Lowlands,
As you lay along the Lowlands low."

Oh, then they picked him up and on the deck he died.
They wound him in his hammock, for it was long and wide;
And they threw him overboard and they sank him in the
    tide,
As they sailed along the Lowlands, Lowlands,
As they sailed along the Lowlands low.

AA

*Mrs. A. R. Blake of White River Junction, Vermont, re-
membered hearing this ballad first some thirty-five years ago
as sung by Mr. Arthur Parks of Hardwick, Vermont, who
worked on a farm in that locality.*

H. H. F., Collector
1935

Structure: A¹ B A² C (2,2,2,2); Rhythm D but divergent;
Contour: undulating; note the large melodic intervals—
sevenths and ninths; Scale: major

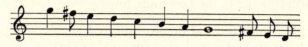

t.c. C.

The Golden Victory

Tr. M. O.

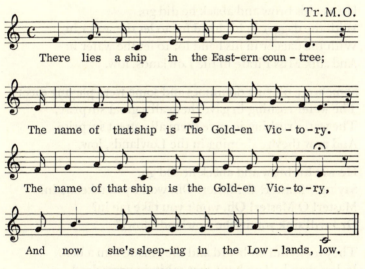

The Golden Victory

There lies a ship in the Eastern countree;
The name of that ship is The Golden Victory.
The name of that ship is The Golden Victory,
And now she's sleeping in the Lowlands, low.

Up jumped the Captain, and up spoke he,
Saying, "Is there anyone on board who can sink the French
        gallee?
Is there anyone on board who can sink the French gallee,
And sink Miss Pirate in the Lowlands, low?"

Up jumped the cabin boy and up spoke he,
Saying, "Master! O Master! Oh, what will you give to me?
Master! O Master! Oh, what will you give to me,
If I will sink her in the Lowlands, low?"

"I'll give you silver, and I'll give you gold,
The hand of my daughter if you'll return bold,
The hand of my daughter if you'll return bold
And sink Miss Pirate in the Lowlands, low."

He wet his brow and aback he did go,
With the dagger in his hand for to let the water in,
With the dagger in his hand for to let the water in
And sink Miss Pirate in the Lowlands, low.

Some were playing dominoes and some were playing dice;
The water rushing in gave them all a great surprise,
The water rushing in gave them all a great surprise,
And now they're sleeping in the Lowlands, low.

He wet his brow and aback he did go,
Saying, "Master! O Master! Oh, won't you take me in?
Master! O Master! Oh, won't you take me in?
Or I will sink you in the Lowlands, low!"

They took him on board and they made him a bed.
In less than half an hour that cabin boy was dead.
In less than half an hour that cabin boy was dead,
And now he's sleeping in the Lowlands, low.

BB

*Mrs. Elmer George of East Calais, Vermont, learned this
version of Child 286 from her parents and from Henry
Laundry.*

H. H. F., *Collector*
1933

Structure: A B A C (4,4,4,4); Rhythm C and D; Contour: undulating; Scale: major

t.c. B flat.

The Golden Victory

Tr. M. O.

1. The good old ship was sail - ing, a -
sail - ing o'er the sea; The name of the
ship was The Gold - en Vic - to - ry; The
name of the ship was The Gold - en Vic - to -
ry as she sailed o'er the Low - lands low.

2. Up jumped the Cap - tain and up spoke
he, "Is there an - y - one on board That will

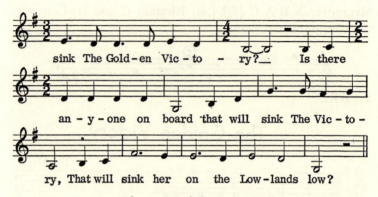

sink The Gold-en Vic-to - ry?__ Is there an - y - one on board that will sink The Vic - to - ry, That will sink her on the Low-lands low?

The Golden Victory

Tr. P. B.

The good old ship was sail - ing, a - sail - ing o'er the sea; The name of this ship was The Gold - en Vic - to - ry. The name of this ship was The Gold - en Vic - to - ry And it sailed on the Low-lands low.

The Golden Victory

The good old ship was sailing, a-sailing o'er the sea;
The name of the ship was The Golden Victory.
The name of the ship was The Golden Victory
As she sailed o'er the Lowlands low.

Up jumped the captain and up spoke he,
"Is there anyone on board that will sink the Golden Vic-
    tory?
Is there anyone on board that will sink the Victory,
That will sink her in the Lowlands low?"

"O Captain, O Captain, oh, what'll you give to me?
O Captain, O Captain, oh, what'll you give to me?
O Captain, O Captain, oh, what'll you give to me
If I sink her down in the Lowlands low?"

"I will give you silver and I will give you gold,
The hand of my daughter if you should return bold,
The hand of my daughter if you should return bold,
If you sink her down in the Lowlands low."

He bent down his breast and away he did swim,
A dagger in his hand for to let the water in,
A dagger in his hand for to let the water in
And to sink her down in the Lowlands low.

He bent upon his back and away went he.
He swam 'til he came to The Golden Victory.
He swam 'til he came to The Golden Victory
For he sank her down in the Lowlands low.

"O Captain, O Captain, oh, will you take me in?"
. . . .
. . . .
. . . .

They took him from the water and they laid him on the bed.
In less than half an hour, this cabing boy was dead.
In less than half an hour, this cabing boy was dead
And they sank him down in the Lowlands low.

CC

As sung by Will Barry of Belvidere, Vermont.

M. Olney, Collector
September 25, 1942

Structure: A¹ B A² C (2,2,2,2); Rhythm D; Contour: undulating; Scale: major

t.c. C.

The French Gallee

The French Gallee

Come, all ye young cabin boys, and listen to me
And I'll sing you the song of the French gallee.

Up spoke the captain and up says he,
"Is there any man on board that will sink the French gallee
And sink Young Pilot in the Lowlands low?"

Up spoke the cabin boy and thus spoke he:
"O Master, O Master, what will you give to me?
O Master, O Master, what will you give to me
If I'll sink them fellows in the Lowlands low?"

"I'll give you silver and I'll give you gold
And the hand of my daughter if you'll return bold
And sink Young Pilot in the Lowlands low."

He bent his breast and away he did swim
With a dagger in his hand for to let the water in,
With a dagger in his hand for to let the water in
And sink them Pilot in the Lowlands low.

Some were playing dominos and more playing chess
And the water rushing in gave them all a great surprise,
And the water rushing in give them all a great surprise,
For they were sinking in the Lowlands low.

He bent his breast and back he did swim,
Saying, "Captain, O Captain, won't you take me in?
Captain, O Captain, won't you take me in?
If you don't, I'll sink you in the Lowlands low."

They took him and they made him a bed;
Less than a half an hour this cabin boy was dead,
Less than a half an hour this cabin boy was dead,
And he was sleeping in the Lowlands low.

DD

As sung by Hanford Hayes of Stacyville, Maine.

M. Olney, Collector
May 10, 1942

Lowlands Low

"Oh, I shall give you silver and I shall give you store,
Likewise my daughter, Nellie, when we do reach the shore
If you'll sink them in the Lowlands, yes, the Lowlands,
If you sink them in the Lowlands, low."

Oh, the boy he took an auger and overboard jumped he;
He swam till he came to The Golden Vanitee.
Oh, he bored a hole once and he bored a hole twice,

He bored a hole so as to let the water in
And it dazzled in their eyes
And he sank them in the Lowlands, yes, the Lowlands,
And he sank them in the Lowlands, low!

Oh, the boy he swam again till he swam to the other side,
Crying, "Captain, pick me up for I fear I will be drowned!
For I'm sinking in the Lowlands, yes, the Lowlands!
I am sinking in the Lowlands, low!"

Oh, the captain being standing all by the starboard side,
"I'll stick you! I'll stab you! I'll send you on the tide!
Yes, I'll sink you in the Lowlands forever and ever more!
I will sink you in the Lowlands, low!"

Oh, his comrades picked him up; it was on the deck he died;
They sewed him in his hammock[1] for it was long and wide
And they sank him in the Lowlands, yes, the Lowlands
And they sank him in the Lowlands, low.

EE

As sung by Daniel Dragon of Ripton, Vermont.

M. Olney, Collector
July 27, 1941

Structure: A¹ B A² C (2,2,2,2); Rhythm D but divergent;
Contour: undulating; Scale: major

t.c. B flat.

The Golden Vanistee

Tr. H. E. F. B.

There is a ship in the North A-mer - i-kee

[1] pronounced "hammick"

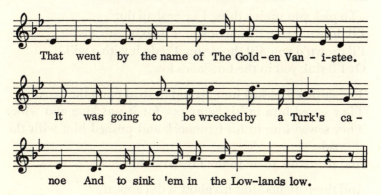

That went by the name of The Gold-en Van - i-stee.

It was going to be wrecked by a Turk's ca -

noe And to sink 'em in the Low-lands low.

The Golden Vanistee

There is a ship in the North Amerikee
That went by the name of The Golden Vanistee.
It was going to be wrecked by a Turk's canoe
And to sink 'em in the Lowlands low.

The first one on deck was a little cabin boy,
Saying, "Captain, what'll you give me if the ship I will
    destroy?"
"Gold I will give you and my daughter for your bride,
If you'll sink her in the Lowlands low."

He grasped for an auger and overboard he jumped;
He bent to his breast and he swum far out to sea;
He bent to his breast and he swum far out to sea,
Till he came to this Turk's canoe.

He out with his instrument already for the use.
He bored in three holes that let in the salty juice;
He bored in three holes that let in the salty juice
And he sunk her in the Lowlands low.

He bent to his breast and he swum back again;
He swum till he came to The Golden Vanistee,
Saying, "Captain, pick me up for I'm growing very weak;
I am sinking in the Lowlands low."

"To pick you up is a thing I ne'er shall do;
I'll drown'd you, I'll shoot you, I'll do it with a will;
I'll drown'd you, I'll shoot you, I'll do it with a will,
Or I'll sink you in the Lowlands low."

The shipmen picked him up and he died upon the deck;
They sewed him in his hammock for it was long and wide;
They sewed him in his hammock and pushed him with the
    tide
And they sunk them in the Lowlands low.

And three nights after his ghost it did appear,
Treating to the captain a glass of lager beer,
A-treating to the captain a glass of lager beer,
And he sunk them in the Lowlands low.

FF

*Sent by George Edwards of Burlington, Vermont. "The
Golden Vanity" was a ballad known and used by his family
for a very long time. Just how long it had been handed down
from generation to generation he did not know.*

H. H. F., Collector
March 28, 1934

Structure: A¹ B A² C D¹ D² (2,2,2,2,2,2); Rhythm D but
divergent; Contour: undulating; Scale: Dorian

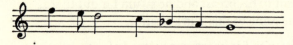

t.c. E.

The Golden Vanity

Tr. M. O.

Sir   Wal - ter Ra - leighbuilt   a   ship   To

sail   the Neth - er - land seas,   Say - ing,

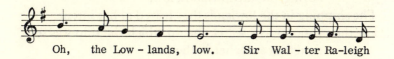

Oh,   the Low - lands, low.   Sir Wal - ter Ra-leigh

built   a ship   to   sail   the Neth - er - land seas

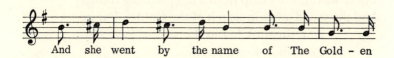

And   she   went   by   the name   of   The Gold - en

Van - i - ty   And they sunk   her in   the Low - lands,

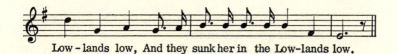

Low - lands low, And they sunk her in   the Low-lands low.

The Golden Vanity

Sir Walter Raleigh built a ship to sail the Netherland seas,
        Saying, oh, the lowlands, low.
Sir Walter Raleigh built a ship to sail the Netherland seas
And she went by the name of the Golden Vanity
        And they sunk her in the

Lowlands, lowlands, low,
And they sunk her in the
Lowlands, low.

The shipping in the lowlands they feared of her intent,
        Saying, oh, the lowlands, low,
The shipping in the lowlands they feared of her intent
For the mission was a secret one on which the ship was sent,
        And they sunk her in the
        Lowlands, lowlands, low,
        And they sunk her in the
        Lowlands, low.

There was another ship from a neighboring country,
        Saying, oh, the lowlands, low,
There was another ship from a neighboring country
And she sailed away in search of the Golden Vanity
        And she sunk her in the
        Lowlands, lowlands, low,
        And she sunk her in the
        Lowlands, low.

She sought the ship for many a day, and went from sea to sea,
        Saying, oh, the lowlands, low,
She sought the ship for many a day, and went from sea to
        sea
Till at length she found her in a port, on the Zuyder Zee,
        And she sunk her in the
        Lowlands, lowlands, low,
        And she sunk her in the
        Lowlands, low.

Then up spake John, a brave young lad, he was the cabin
        boy,
        Saying, oh, the lowlands, low,
Then up spake John, a brave young lad, he was the cabin
        boy

And he said to the captain, "I can that ship destroy,"
"I can sink her in the
Lowlands, lowlands, low,
I can sink her in the
Lowlands, low."

You are brave, my lad," the captain said, as brave, as brave
can be,"
Saying, oh, the lowlands, low,
You are brave, my lad," the captain said, as brave, as brave
can be,
And a rich reward awaits you and I will pay you fee
If you'll sink her in the
Lowlands, lowlands, low,
If you'll sink her in the
Lowlands, low."

Then Johnny he made ready and he plunged into the sea,
Saying, oh, the lowlands, low,
Then Johnny he made ready and he plunged into the sea
And he swam to the side of the Golden Vanity,
And he sunk her in the
Lowlands, lowlands, low,
And he sunk her in the
Lowlands, low.

Then Johnny had a tool that was fitted for the spoil,
Saying, oh, the lowlands, low,
Then Johnny had a tool that was fitted for the spoil
And in the bottom low he bored the fatal hole,
And he sunk her in the
Lowlands, lowlands, low,
And he sunk her in the
Lowlands, low.

Then Johnny he swam back and was taken up on board,
Saying, oh, the lowlands, low,

Then Johnny he swam back and was taken up on board
And was greeted by his shipmates and given great accord,
     For he sunk her in the
     Lowlands, lowlands, low,
     For he sunk her in the
     Lowlands, low.

A leave of absence, for a year, was granted John with pay,
     Saying, oh, the lowlands, low,
A leave of absence, for a year, was granted John with pay,
And the rich reward of gold and fee was given him that day,
     For he sunk her in the
     Lowlands, lowlands, low,
     For he sunk her in the
     Lowlands, low.

GG

As recited by Miss Maude Lyman Stevens of Newport, Rhode Island. Miss Stevens says, "This was recited to me many years ago by a woman who learned it from an English friend." She stated she had never heard it sung.

M. Olney, Collector
October 25, 1945

The Golden Vanity

There was a gallant ship and a gallant ship was she,
     High diddle-dee as the winds blow low,
And her name it was The Golden Vanity[1]
And she sailed for the Lowlands low, heigh-O,
And she sailed for the Lowlands low.

She had not been many days at sea,
     High diddle-dee as the winds blow low,
When bearing down upon her came a French gallee

[1] Pronounced *Van-i-tee.*

As she sailed for the Lowlands low, heigh-O,
As she sailed for the Lowlands low.

Then up spoke the captain of The Golden Vanity,
       High diddle-dee as the winds blow low,
"Which shall be his reward who will sink the French gallee
And get safe to the Lowlands low, heigh-O,
And get safe to the Lowlands low."

Then up spoke the middy of The Golden Vanity,
       High diddle-dee as the winds blow low,
"What will be my reward if I sink the French gallee,
And get safe to the Lowlands low, heigh-O,
And get safe to the Lowlands low?"

Then up spoke the captain of the Golden Vanity,
       High diddle-dee as the winds blow low,
"We will give you an estate in the North Countree
When we come from the Lowlands low, heigh-O,
When we come from the Lowlands low."

They wrapped him up in a boat's skin,
       High diddle-dee as the winds blow low,
And threw him overboard to let him sink or swim
And set sail for the Lowlands low, heigh-O,
And set sail for the Lowlands low.

He turned him around in the raging sea,
       High diddle-dee as the winds blow low,
And soon came up to the French gallee
As she sailed for the Lowlands low, heigh-O,
As she sailed for the Lowlands low.

The Frenchmen were playing at cards and dice,
       High diddle-dee as the winds blow low,
When he pulled out an instrument and sent them in a trice
And they never reached the Lowlands low, heigh-O,
And they never reached the Lowlands low.

He turned him around in the raging seas,
> High diddle-dee as the winds blow low,
And soon came up with The Golden Vanity
As she sailed for the Lowlands low, heigh-O,
As she sailed for the Lowlands low.

"Now throw me a rope and take me up on board,"
> High diddle-dee as the winds blow low,
"And prove to me as good as your word
When we come from the Lowlands low, heigh-O,
When we come from the Lowlands low."

"No, no," said the captain, "we want you not on board,"
> High diddle-dee as the winds blow low;
"Now we will prove as good as our word
When we come from the Lowlands low, heigh-O,
When we come from the Lowlands low."

"Then just as I served the French gallee,"
> High diddle-dee as the winds blow low,
"Just so will I serve The Golden Vanity.
I shall never reach the Lowlands low, heigh-O;
I shall never reach the Lowlands low."

So they threw a rope and took him up on board,
> High diddle-dee as the winds blow low,
And proved to him much better than their word
When they came from the Lowlands low, heigh-O,
When they came from the Lowlands low.

The gallant middy was never so happy in his life,
> High diddle-dee as the winds blow low,
As when he got the daughter of the captain for his wife,
When he came from the Lowlands low, heigh-O,
When he came from the Lowlands low.

HH

As printed in JAF, *XVIII, 125, with the headnote, " 'The*
Little Cabin Boy' Recorded January 13, 1905, by M. E. B.,

Irasburg, Vt., from the singing of an aged man born in Glover, Vt." (A note from Mr. Barry to H. H. F. indicates that the singer was Solon Percival.)

Phillips Barry, Collector
January 13, 1905

Structure: A B C (sequence) D E F (2,2,2,2,2,2); Rhythm D; Contour: undulating (note the octave leaps); Scale: major

t.c. C.

The Little Cabin Boy

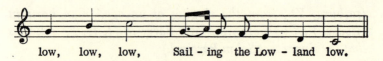

low,   low,   low,   Sail - ing the Low - land low.

The Little Cabin Boy

There was a ship in the Northern Countrie,
All in the Lowland low,
The name of the ship was the "Gold China Tree,"
All in the Lowland low, low, low.
Sailing the Lowland, low, low, low,
Sailing the Lowland low.

She had not sailed past leagues two or three,
All in the Lowland low
She had not sailed past leagues two or three
Before she espied a French Galilee.

The first that spoke was the ship Captain's man,
All in the Lowland low,
Saying, "Master, O Master, we're all undone,
All in the Lowland, low, low, low!"

Next spoke up was the little Cabin Boy,
All in the Lowland low,
Saying, "Master, O Master, what will you give to me,
If I will sink the French Galilee?"

"Oh, I will give you gold, and I will give you fee,
All in the Lowland low,
And my eldest daughter your bride shall be,
All in the Lowland low, low, low."

He smote upon his breast, and away swung he,
All in the Lowland low,
He smote upon his breast, and away swung he,
And he swung till he came to the French Galilee.

Then he espied a little augur that came from a nun,
All in the Lowland low,
Then he espied a little auger that came from a nun,
And bored holes with it, twenty and one.

Some threw their hats, and some threw their caps,
All in the Lowland low,
Saying "For the Lord's sake, stop up the salt water gaps!
All in the Lowland low, low, low!"

He smote upon his breast, and away swung he,
All in the Lowland low,
He smote upon his breast, and away swung he,
Until he came to the "Gold China Tree."

Then all around the ship this little boy did swim,
All in the Lowland low,
Saying, "Master, O Master, won't you take me in?
Or I'll serve you as I've served them!"

They threw out a rope, and they slightly drew him in,
All in the Lowland low,
They threw out a rope, and they slightly drew him in,
And then he began to dance and sing,

Saying, "Master, O Master, what will you give to me,
All in the Lowland low,
Saying, Master, O Master, what will you give to me?
For I have sunk the French Galilee!"

"Oh, I'll give you gold, and I'll give you fee,
All in the Lowland low,
Oh I'll give you gold, and I'll give you fee,
And I'll give you the land of North Amerikee!"

"Oh, I'll have none of your gold, or none of your fee,
All in the Lowland low,
Oh, I'll have none of your gold, or none of your fee,
But your eldest daughter my bride shall be!"

He married the daughter in spite of them all,
All in the Lowland low,
He married the daughter in spite of them all,
May the Devil take the Captain, sailors and all!

II

Sent by Mrs. Forest A. Elkins, 113 Willington Avenue, Stafford Springs, Conn. She wrote, "My father, James P. Angell, from whom I learned it, was born in Rhode Island and was a descendant of Thomas Angell who came with Roger Williams to settle Rhode Island, and he learned the song from his mother, who was a Brown, another pioneer family of Rhode Island. As far as I can figure out, the song has been known in our family one hundred and ten years at least."

H. H. F., Collector
August 4, 1931

Bold Gallantry

I have a ship in my own country.
It goes by the name of some Bold Gallantry.
I fear she will be taken by some Turkish galoo
As she sails along the lowlands, lowlands, lowlands,
As she sails along the lowlands, low.

Up steps a boy, to the captain did say,
"What will you give to me if her I'll destroy?"
"I will give you gold and I will give you store
And you shall have my daughter dear
When you arrive on shore
If you'll sink her in the lowlands, lowlands, lowlands,
If you'll sink her in the lowlands, low."

This boy had an auger he'd brought from the shore.
Instead of boring one hole, 'twould bore twenty-four.
While some were playing cards and others shaking dice,

He let the water in and he dazzled all their lives
And he sank them in the lowlands, lowlands, lowlands,
And he sank them in the lowlands, low.

This boy he won gold and silver bright,
This boy he won gold and silver bright,
This boy he won gold and silver bright,
Likewise the captain's daughter
Who was his heart's delight,
For he sank her in the lowlands, lowlands, lowlands,
For he sank her in the lowlands, low.

JJ

*As sung by Mrs. Lily Delorme of Cadyville, New York,
whose family was born in and came from Starksboro, Vermont.*

M. Olney, Collector
June 8, 1942

The Green Willow Tree

There was a little ship that sailed o'er the sea
And she went by the name of The Green Willow Tree,
As she sail-ed in the low, as she sail-ed in the low,
As she sail-ed in the Lowlands low.

There was another ship that sailed o'er the sea
And she went by the name of The Turkish Revelee
Lying anchored in the low, lying anchored in the low,
Lying anchored in the Lowlands low.

"O Captain, O Captain, oh, what will you give me
If I will sink that Turkish Revelee
Lying anchored in the low, lying anchored in the low,
Lying anchored in the Lowlands low?"

"Oh, I will give you gold and I will give you fee,
Likewise my oldest daughter in North Amerikee,
If you'll sink them in the low, if you'll sink them in the low,
If you'll sink them in the Lowlands low.

He had a little auger all fitted for the use
To bore four and twenty holes all at one push,
As he sank them in the low, as he sank them in the low,
As he sank them in the Lowlands low.

Some were playing cards and some were playing dice.
They all were playing at the devil's own advice
As he sank them in the low, as he sank them in the low,
As he sank them in the Lowlands low.

Some run with hats and some run with caps
Trying to stop up the salt water gaps
As he sank them in the low, as he sank them in the low,
As he sank them in the Lowlands low.

"O Captain, O Captain, oh, take me on board,
And do unto me as good as your word,
Since I've sunk them in the low, since I've sunk them in the
        low,
Since I've sunk them in the Lowlands low."

"Oh, no, I will not take you on board
Nor do unto you as good as my word
Since you've sunk them in the low, since you've sunk them
        in the low,
Since you've sunk them in the Lowlands low."

"O Captain, O Captain, if you don't take me in
I'll serve you the same as I've just served them.
I will sink you in the low, I will sink you in the low,
I will sink you in the Lowlands low."

'Twas then this cruel captain he took him on board
And did unto him as good as his word,
Since he'd sunk them in the low, since he'd sunk them in the
    low,
Since he'd sunk them in the Lowlands low.

Captain Ward and the Rainbow
(Child 287)

"Captain Ward and the Rainbow" gives an account, probably accurate, of the efforts of the King to capture John Ward of Kent sometime between 1604 and 1609. Ward and a Dutch accomplice named Dansekar had become pirates about 1604 by persuading the crew of one of the King's ships to follow them in a career of buccaneering. Ward was captured and hanged before 1610, but evidently not until he had defeated a ship called *The Rainbow* sent to take him. *The Rainbow* was the name of one of Drake's boats at Cadiz in 1587, and "the three lost jewels" that the King feels would have brought proud Ward to him (see Child) were the Earls of Essex and Cumberland and Lord Mountjoy, all dead by 1606.

Phillips Barry, *British Ballads from Maine,* 358–63, devotes a good bit of discussion to the British and American versions of the story. His C text tells of the eventual capture and hanging of Ward and may recall the final undoing of the pirate who had previously eluded his King. More common, though, is the escape ending which is pretty much like that on "Sir Andrew Barton" (Child 167/250). At any rate, the King's ship is always *The Rainbow,* whether successful or routed, and Ward, if he escapes in the ballad, was later to be hanged.

Both Flanders texts are similar to *The Forget-me-not Songster* version printed by Turner and Fisher in Philadelphia and by Nafis and Cornish in New York. This form of the song was also included in *The Pearl Songster* (New York) and in *The Forecastle Songster* (New York, 1849) and is not unlike the seventeenth-century Child version. Flanders A leaves off the lines about "the three lost jewels" who might have captured Ward. Flanders B is poorly recalled.

See Coffin, 154–7 (American) and Greig and Keith, 239–40 (Scottish) for a start on a bibliography. Barry, *op. cit.*, 251–8, prints a sampling of the songster versions cited above and a Coverly (Boston) broadside.

A

This song is copied literatim et punctatim from The Green Mountain Songster, *compiled by a Revolutionary soldier of Sandgate, Vermont, in 1823. The book is now in the possession of Harold Rugg, assistant librarian of the Dartmouth College Library. Printed in* Vermont Folk-Songs & Ballads, *242.*

H. H. F., Collector
1931

Captain Ward and the Rain-Bow

Come all you jolly seamen bold, that live by tuck of drum,
I'll tell you of a rank robber, now on the seas is come,
His name is called Captain Ward, as you the truth shall hear,
There's not been such a robber found out this hundred years.

He wrote a letter to our King on the fifth of January,
To see if he would take him in and all his jolly company,
To see if he would accept of him and his jolly seamen bold,
'Twas for a ransom, he would give two thousand pounds in
   gold.

O he's deceived the King of France, likewise the King of
   Spain,

And how should he prove true to me, for he proved false to
    them?
O no, O no, then says our king, no such a thing shall be,
For he hath been a rank robber and rover on the sea.

Well then, my boys, says Captain Ward, we'll put to sea
    again,
To see what shipping we can take, on the coast of France or
    Spain:
O there they spied a lofty ship a sailing from the west,
Laden with Silks and Sattins, and Cambrics of the best.

Then they bore down to her straightway, they thinking no
    such thing,
They robb'd them of their merchandize, and bid them tell
    their king;
Now when our king did hear of it, his heart was griev'd full
    sore,
To think his shipping could not pass as they had done
    before.

The King he built a worthy ship, a worthy ship of fame,
The Rainbow was she called, the Rainbow was her name;
He rigged her, and freighted her, and sent her to the sea,
With a hundred and fifty mariners to bear her company.

They sailed east, they sailed west, but nothing could espy—
At length they came to the very spot where Captain Ward
    did lie:
Who is the owner of that ship, the Rainbow then did cry?
O here I am, said Captain Ward, let no man me deny.

Why lie you here, you ugly dog, you cowardly wanton thief?
What makes you lie at anchor, and keep our king in grief?
You lie, you lie, said Captain Ward, so true as I hear you lie,
For I never robb'd an Englishman, as Englishman but they.

As for these worthy Scotchmen, I love them as my own,
My greatest joy and heart's delight's to pull the French and
   Spaniards down;
Why say thou so, you bold robber, we'll soon humble your
   pride,
And then they fir'd with their great guns, and gave Ward a
   broadside.

Fire on, fire on, said Captain Ward, I value you not a pin,
If you are brass on the outside, I am good steel within;
Fight on, fight on, said Captain Ward, the sport well pleases
   me
And if you fight this month or more your captain I will be.

They fought from eight in the morning, till twelve o'clock
   at night
At length the royal Rainbow began to take her flight;
Go home Says Captain Ward, go tell your King from me,
If he reigns king upon dry land, I reign king on the sea.

B

As sung by Ralph Lewis, Agamenticus Section, York, Maine.
Learned from his grandfather. Printed in Ballads Migrant
in New England, *204.*

M. *Olney, Collector*
September 22, 1947

Structure: A B^a1 B^2 B^a1 (4,4,4,4); Rhythm B; Contour: undulating; Scale: Mixolydian

t.c. B flat.

For mel. rel. see BES, 348 B (distant).

Captain Ward and the Rainbow

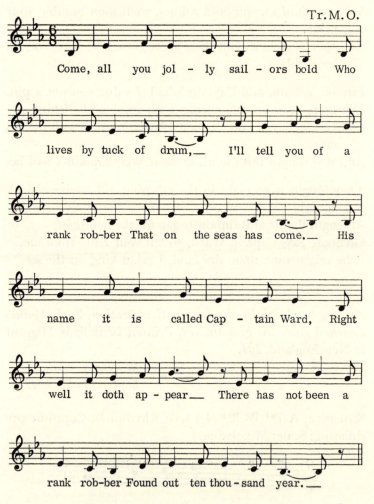

Tr. M. O.

Come, all you jol - ly sail - ors bold Who lives by tuck of drum,— I'll tell you of a rank rob-ber That on the seas has come.— His name it is called Cap - tain Ward, Right well it doth ap - pear— There has not been a rank rob-ber Found out ten thou - sand year.—

Captain Ward and the Rainbow

Come, all you jolly sailors bold
Who lives by tuck of drum,

I'll tell you of a rank robber
That on the seas has come.
His name it is called Captain Ward.
Right well it doth appear
There has not been a rank robber
Found out ten thousand year.

He wrote a letter to a king,
On the first of January,
To see if he could accept of him
And all his jolly company.
And for a ransom he would pay
Ten thousand pounds in gold.
"Oh no, oh no," then said the King,
"For no such thing can be,
For you have been a rank robber,
A rover on the sea.

"For you deceived the King of France
And then the King of Spain.
For how can you prove true to us
When you proved false to them?"
Then says Captain Ward, "My boys,
We put to sea again
To see what prizes we can find
On the coast of France and Spain."

They sailed East, they sailed West
(*can't think*)
They espied a lofty ship
A-sailing from the West
Loaded with silks and satins
And cambrics of the best.
Then they bore down on her,
A-thinking of no such thing.
They robbed them of their merchandise
And bid them tell the King.

And when the King did hear of this
His heart was grief full sore
To think his ships would not get pass
And as they had done before.
The King caused the old

. . . .

And a worthy ship of fame.
The Rainbow she was called
And The Rainbow was her home.

He rigged her and he freighted her
And sent her to the sea,
With fully five hundred brave mariners
To bear her company.
They sailed East and they sailed West
But nothing did they spy
Till they came to the very spot
Where Captain Ward did lie.
"Who is the owner of that ship?"
The Rainbow then did cry.

That the gallant Rainbow shot out on either side.
"Fire on, fire on," said Captain Ward,
"We value not a pin.
If you be brass on the outside
We are good steel within!"

We shot and shot in the morning
Shot and shot in vain . . . .

The Mermaid

(Child 289)

It is an established belief among sailors that it is unhappy to sail on Friday and that mermaids both bode bad weather and lead ships to destruction. The ship in "The Mermaid" is therefore doomed. It goes down, carrying the crew to Davy Jones's locker. In Child's A text, the tragedy of the voyage is retained, though a bit sentimentally; however, in the Child B–D series the mood lightens and nobody seems to care very much. American versions, with their "stormy winds" refrain, follow this B–D tradition and are generally close to print and full of spirit. This is undoubtedly because of the popularity of the ballad in college songbooks and in the music halls of Britain and America during the last 150 years. See Coffin, 158, for a start on the extensive bibliography to such material. He also gives references to the game-song and play-party uses to which the ballad has been put.

Dean–Smith, 88, and Belden, 101 (English), and Greig and Keith, 242, and Ord, 333–4 (Scottish) include British citations. Coffin, 157, gives a list of texts from oral tradition in America. The Flanders material and all but one of the versions referred to there are much alike.

The three tunes for Child 289 are related, but fairly distantly.

271

A

Mrs. Ellen M. Sullivan of Springfield, Vermont, remem-
bered this song.

H. H. F., Collector
August 15, 1932

Structure: A B C D (4,4,4,4); Rhythm C and D but divergent; Contour: undulating; Scale: major

t.c. A flat.

For mel. rel. see DV, 602, No. 48 (B); FCB4, 124 (distant);
Sharp 1, 293 C and D.

Tr. M. O.

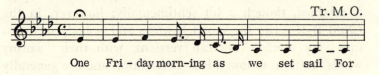

One Fri - day morn-ing as   we   set sail For

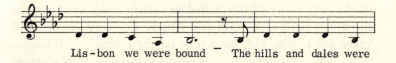

Lis - bon we were bound ⁀ The hills and dales were

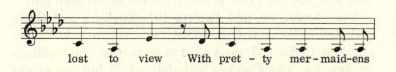

lost   to   view   With pret - ty   mer - maid-ens

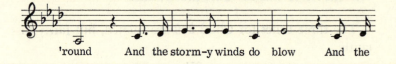

'round   And the storm-y winds do   blow   And the

One Friday morning as we set sail—
For Lisbon we were bound—
The hills and dales were lost to view
With pretty mermaidens 'round.

Refrain: And the stormy winds do blow
        And the raging seas do roar
        And we poor sailors are bound for the top
        While the landsmen do lie down below, down below.

Then out spoke the capting of our gallant ship,
No braver man could be,
Saying, "I have a wife in Dublintown
Who this night a widow will be."

(Repeat refrain after each stanza.)

Then out spoke a boy of our gallant ship,
And a gallant lad was he,
Saying, "I've got a mother in Dublintown
Who this night will look for me."

Out spoke the cook of our gallant ship,
And a very good cook was he,
Saying, "I care more for my kettles and my pans
Than all of the depths of the sea."

Then out spoke the mate of our gallant ship,
And a gallant man was he,
Saying, "I have a sweetheart in Dublintown
Who tonight will weep for me."

And three times around went our gallant ship,
And three times around went she;
Then three times around went our gallant ship
And she sank to the depths of the sea.

B

*As sung by Charles A. Greene of Woodstock, Vermont.
Learned when a young man.*

M. Olney, Collector
June 2, 1941

The Gallant Ship

One Friday morn as we set sail,
And we were not far from land
When the captain 'spied a pretty fair maid,
With a comb and a glass in her hand.

*Then something about a storm. They realized they were
helpless, when:*

Then first spoke the captain of our gallant ship,
A fine spoken man was he,
Saying, "I have a wife in fair Yorkshire town,
And a widow I fear she will be."

Then up spoke the mate of our gallant ship,
A fine spoken man was he,

Saying, "I have a sweetheart in fair Dublin town
And tonight she'll be looking for me."

Then up spoke the cook of our gallant ship,
And a very fine cook was he,
Saying, "I care more for my kettles and my pans
Than all of the depths of the sea."

Then up spoke the cabin boy of our gallant ship,
A fine spoken lad was he,
Saying, "I have a mother in a fair Vermont town
Who this night is praying for,
Who this night is praying for me."

Then three times 'round went our gallant ship,
And three times 'round went she,
And three times 'round went our gallant ship
And she sank to the bottom of the sea.

C

Mailed to H. H. F. by Mrs. Sarah Taylor, New Bedford, Massachusetts, as sung by Ulysses S. Jessup of Scotland, Connecticut. Copied literatim et punctatim.

H. H. F., Collector
January, 1951

The Mermaid

It was on a Friday's evening
That gallant ship did sail
And we not far from shore
The first we came across
Was the Captain of our ship,
And a well spoken man was he,
I have a wife in New York City,
And to night she'll be weeping for me

Chorus

Oh blow you winds oh blow
While we poor sailors go skipping from the tops,

And the land lubbers lie down below below below
And the land lubbers lie down below.

The next we came across was two sailors of the ship,
And two well spoken boys were they.
We have a father and a mother in New York City
And to night they'll be weeping for us.

(Chorus)

The next we came across was the cook of our ship
And a black old devil was she,
I care much more for my kettles and my pots,
Than I do for the rolling of the sea.

(Chorus)

Then three times around went our noble gallant ship,
And three times around went she
Then three times around went our noble gallant ship
'Till she sank to the bottom of the sea.

Chorus

D

*As sung by Daniel Howells of Providence, Rhode Island.
Learned when a boy in England where he was born.*

*M. Olney, Collector
January 27, 1945*

Structure: A B C D¹ D² (2,2,2,2,2); Rhythm C; Contour:
undulating; Scale: major

t.c. D.

For mel. rel. see Sharp 1, 293, C and D; DV, 602, No. 48
(B); RO1, 203.

The Mermaid

Tr. H. E. F. B.

Oh, one Fri-day morn when we set sail And our
ship not far from land, We there did es-py a
pret-ty mer-maid With a comb and a glass in her
hand, oh, in her hand, With a comb and a glass
in her hand, While the rag-ing seas did roar And the
storm - y wynds did blow, While we jol-ly sail-ors
were a - sit-ting up a - loft, And the
land - lub-bers ly - ing down be - low, be - low, be - low,
And the land - lub-bers ly - ing down be - low.

The Mermaid

Oh, one Friday morn when we set sail
And our ship not far from land,
We there did espy a pretty mermaid
With a comb and a glass in her hand, oh, in her hand,
With a comb and a glass in her hand,
While the raging seas did roar,
And the stormy wynds did blow,
While we jolly sailors were a-sitting up aloft,
And the landlubbers lying down below, below, below,
And the landlubbers lying down below.

(*Repeat refrain after each stanza as indicated.*)

Oh, then up starts the cook of our gallant ship,
And a gruff old soul was he.
"Oh, I have a wife in fair Plymouth-town,
But a widow I fear that she will be, that she will be,
But a widow I fear she will be."
And the raging seas did roar, *etc.*

And up spoke the little cabin boy,
And a pretty little boy was he.
"Oh, I am more grieved for my daddy and my mammy
Than you for your wives all three, all three, all three,
Than you for your wives all three."
And the raging seas did roar, *etc.*

Then three times 'round went our gallant ship,
And three times 'round went she.
For the want of a lifeboat they all went down,
And she sank to the bottom of the sea, the sea, the sea,
And she sank to the bottom of the sea.
While the raging seas did roar, *etc.*

E

Recorded by Phillips Barry from the singing of J. G. Marcy, Newbury, Vermont, and published in JAF, XVIII, 136, with its tune.

Phillips Barry, Collector
October 11, 1904

Structure: A¹ B¹ A² B² (2,2,2,2); Rhythm C and D; Contour: each line an arc; Scale: pentachordal

t.c. E.

For mel. rel. see BES, 365 (distant).

The Mermaid

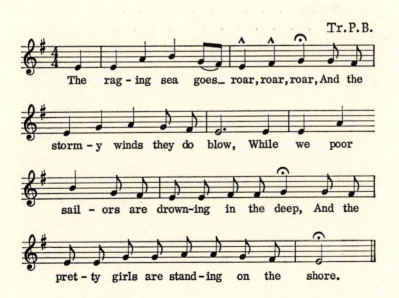

The Mermaid

The first came up was the carpenter of the ship,
    And a hearty old fellow was he,
Saying, "I have a wife in Old England,
    And a widow I'm afraid she will be!"

Refrain:

For the raging sea goes roar, roar, roar,
    And the stormy winds they do blow,
While we poor sailors are drowning in the deep,
    And the pretty girls are standing on the shore.

The next came up was a little cabin boy,
    And a nice little fellow was he,
Saying,—"I'd give more for my daddy and my ma,
    Than I would for your wives all three!"

The next came up was a fair pretty maid,
    With a comb and a glass in her hand,
Saying, ...
     . . . .

John of Hazelgreen

(Child 293)

The full story of "John of Hazelgreen" is given by Child, V, 160, as follows:

A gentleman overhears a damsel making moan for Sir John of Hazelgreen. After some compliment on his part, and some slight information on hers, he tells her that Hazelgreen is married; then there is nothing for her to do, she says, but to hold her peace and die for him. The gentleman proposes that she shall let Hazelgreen go, marry his eldest son, and be made a gay lady; she is too mean a maid for that, and, anyway, had rather die for the object of her affection. Still she allows the gentleman to take her up behind him on his horse and to buy clothes for her at Biggar, though all the time dropping tears for Hazelgreen. After shopping, they mount again, and at last they come to the gentleman's place, when the son runs out to welcome his father. The son is young Hazelgreen, who takes the maid in his arms and kisses off the still-falling tears. The father declares that the two shall be married the next day, and the young man shall have the family lands.

The song was once fairly popular in Britain and America, but in forms that appear close to print and that are usually fragmentary. It has been found much more frequently in the Southeast than elsewhere in this country. Nevertheless, Phillips Barry, *British Ballads from Maine*, 369, prints a rather

unique text from New Brunswick. In it the hero is called
Willie and the story is fragmentary. The Flanders version
is somewhat similar to this text, especially in the second and
third stanzas, but it is even less complete.

The song has been discussed frequently, partly because
Sir Walter Scott composed his "Jock of Hazeldean" by com-
pleting a fragmentary version. The J version in Arthur Kyle
Davis's *Traditional Ballads of Virginia* (Cambridge, Mass.,
1929) shows how the poem and the traditional texts of the
ballad have intermingled. See also BFSSNE, III, 9; Maurice
Kelley's article in *MLN*, XLVI, 304; and Davis, *op. cit.*, 529,
for remarks along this line.

"John of Hazelgreen" is not listed in Dean–Smith. However, Coffin, 158 (American) and Greig and Keith, 244–5
(Scottish) offer a small number of references.

*As sung by Mrs. Lily Delorme of Cadyville, New York. Mrs.
Delorme was born in Schuyler Falls, New York, in 1869. Her
father was born in Starksboro, Vermont; her mother, in
Schuyler Falls, New York. This ballad was learned in her
home as a child. Published in* Ballads Migrant in New England, *237.*

M. Olney, Marjorie Porter, Collectors
December 4, 1941

Structure: A^1 A^1 B A^2 (4,4,4,4); Rhythm B; Contour: arc;
Scale: major

t.c. G.

For mel. rel. see DV, 604 No. 49 (D).

Young Johnny of Hazelgreen

Tr. M. O.

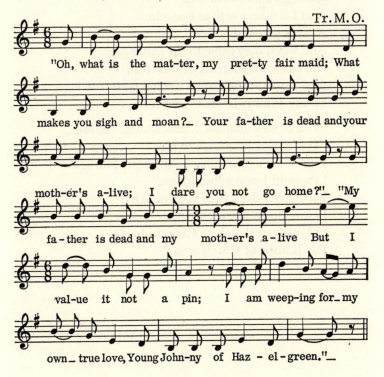

"Oh, what is the mat-ter, my pret-ty fair maid; What makes you sigh and moan?_ Your fa-ther is dead and your moth-er's a-live; I dare you not go home?"_ "My fa-ther is dead and my moth-er's a-live But I val-ue it not a pin; I am weep-ing for_ my own_ true love, Young John-ny of Haz - el - green."_

Young Johnny of Hazelgreen

"Oh, what is the matter, my pretty fair maid;
What makes you sigh and moan?
Your father is dead and your mother's alive;
I dare you not go home?"
"My father is dead and my mother's alive
But I value it not a pin.
I am weeping for my own true love,
Young Johnny of Hazelgreen."

"Come, go with me, my pretty fair maid,
Come go along with me,
And I'll take you to as fine a lord
As ever you wish to see."
And when they came to the castle-gate,
Such a crowd there ne'er was seen,
And amongst the crowd was her own true love,
Young Johnny of Hazelgreen.

"You're welcome back, dear father," he said,
"You're welcome back to me;
You've brought me back my bonny fair bride
I thought I never should see,"
For twenty-five kisses he gave to her
Before he let her in, saying,
"I hope you'll make a virtuous bride
For Johnny of Hazelgreen."

The Irish Lady, or Sally from London
(Laws P9, related to Child 295)

Child, V, 166, gives the story of "The Brown Girl" as follows:

> A young man who has been attached to a girl sends her
> word by letter that he cannot fancy her because she is so
> brown (he has left her for another). She sends a disdainful
> reply. He writes again that he is dangerously ill (he is love-
> sick), and begs her to come quickly and give him back his
> faith. She takes her time in going, and when she comes to
> the sick man's bedside, cannot stand for laughing. She has,
> however, brought a white wand with her, which she
> strokes on his breast, in sign that she gives him back the
> faith which he had given her. But as to forgiving and for-
> getting, that she will never do; she will dance upon his
> grave.

There are not traditional versions of this ballad in America.
However, a song much like "The Brown Girl" and usually
called something similar to "The Irish Lady" or "Sally from
London" has had great popularity in Britain and this country. It derives from broadsides of the eighteenth and nineteenth centuries; in it, the sexes of the lovers are reversed,
the brown complexion of the girl is not mentioned, and
"Are you the doctor?" lines are almost always present. Nor-
mally, it ends with the death of the girl, but a great many
minor variations occur in the plot.

Texts with a happy ending, like A and B below, have

been found in New England (Phillips Barry, *British Ballads from Maine,* 418) and in Michigan (Emelyn E. Gardner and Geraldine J. Chickering, *Ballads and Songs of Southern Michigan,* Ann Arbor, 1939, 150). They seem to derive from the printed versions that relate to the Boston broadside reproduced in Barry, *op. cit.,* 424, although that text is not particularly close to any of the ones mentioned above.

The song is also frequently found containing material in common with other ballads, such as "Glenlogie" (Child 238); "Barbara Allen" (Child 84); "The Death of Queen Jane" (Child 170); "Clerk Saunders" (Child 69); "The Unquiet Grave" (Child 78); "Sweet William's Ghost" (Child 77); and "Lord Thomas and Fair Annet" (Child 73). See Coffin, 159–61, for discussion and an American bibliography. Dean–Smith, 56, and Belden, 111, give English references. Laws, *ABBB,* 252–3, treats the entire tradition and includes a great many Anglo–American citations.

A

Sung by Asa Davis of Milton, Vermont, as learned from his father, Joel Davis, who was born in Duxbury, Vermont.

M. Olney, Collector
July 21, 1946

Pretty Sally

Some hundreds, some hundreds, some hundreds of years,
I courted a lady, a lady so fair;
She being a lady so lofty and high,
That upon this man she could scarce cast her eye.
Lie-fel, a-liddle-lary,
Lie-fel, a-liddle-lary,
Sing torrel-o-day.

"O Sally, O Sally, O Sally," said he,
"I'm sorry that your love and mine can't agree,

But I have no great doubt but my ruin you prove,
Except all your hatred being turned into love."
Lie-fel, a-liddle-lary,
Lie-fel, a-liddle-lary,
Sing torrel-o-day.

"Oh, no, I don't hate you nor no other man,
But as for to love you is more than I can;
Now drop your intentions and end all discourse
For I'll never, never have you, excepting I'm forced."
Lie-fel, a-liddle-lary,
Lie-fel, a-liddle-lary,
Sing torrel-o-day.

Six months being over, a story we hear.
She went for this young man who she lov-ed so dear;
She sent for this young man whom she slighted before,
For her heart it was wounded and she knew not what for.
Lie-fel, a-liddle-lary,
Lie-fel, a-liddle-lary,
Sing torrel-o-day.

She sent for this young man all to her bedside.
"Is the pain in your head, love; is the pain in your side?"
"Oh, no," says the lady, "the pain you ain't guessed
For the pain that torments me, love, lies in my breast."
Lie-fel, a-liddle-lary,
Lie-fel, a-liddle-lary,
Sing torrel-o-day.

"Oh, am I your doctor?" this young man replied,
"Or am I that young man that you once denied?"
"Oh, you are the man that can kill or can cure
And without your assistance I'm ruined I'm sure."
Lie-fel, a-liddle-lary,
Lie-fel, a-liddle-lary,
Sing torrel-o-day.

"O Sally, O Sally, O Sally," said he,
"Oh, don't you remember how you slighted me?
When a question I'd ask you, you'd answer with scorn;
And now I'll reward you of things past and gone."
Lie-fel, a-liddle-lary,
Lie-fel, a-liddle-lary,
Sing torrel-o-day.

"Of things past and gone, love, I hope you'll forgive
And grant me some longer, some longer to live."
"I never'll forgive you which during my breath,
But I'll dance on your grave, love, when you lie under earth!"
Lie-fel, a-liddle-lary,
Lie-fel, a-liddle-lary,
Sing torrel-o-day.

"Farewell to my friends and farewell to my foes;
Farewell to this young man who caused my woes.
I would freely forgive him although he won't me;
Ten thousand times over my follies I see."
Lie-fel, a-liddle-lary,
Lie-fel, a-liddle-lary,
Sing torrel-o-day.

"Farewell to my foes and farewell to my friends;
Farewell to this young man—God make him a man!"
Off from her fingers she took diamond rings three,
Saying, "Wear these for my sake, love, when you're dancing
        over me!"
Lie-fel, a-liddle-lary,
Lie-fel, a-liddle-lary,
Sing torrel-o-day.

"Cheer up, my pretty Sally, and married we'll be.
Then we'll live together in sweet u-ni-tee."
Come, all ye fair maidens, your sweethearts don't slight;
Come, all ye that are pretty girls, for I wish you good night.

Lie-fel, a-liddle-lary,
Lie-fel, a-liddle-lary,
Sing torrel-o-day.

B

This song is copied literatim from The Green Mountain
Songster, *compiled by an old Revolutionary soldier of Sandgate, Vermont, in 1823. The book is now in the possession
of Harold Rugg, Assistant Librarian of the Dartmouth College Library. Printed in* Vermont Folk-Songs & Ballads, *244.*

H. H. F., Collector
1931

The Fair Damsel From London

There was a fair damsel, from London she came,
Her name it was Sally, O Sally by name,
Her riches were more than the king could possess,
And her beauty was more than her riches would fetch.

There was a young lord, one night he did steer
To court this fair damsel with thousands a year;
She being so lofty, her portion so high,
That upon this young man she would scarce cast an eye.

"O Sally, O Sally, O Sally," said he,
"I'm sorry that your love and mine can't agree;
Forever more my ruin you'll prove,
Unless that your hatred be turned into love."

"No hatred to you nor to no other man,
But to say that I love you I'm sure I never can;
So drop your intention and end the discourse,
For I never will marry you unless I am forc'd."

Five or six weeks being over and past,
We heard of this fair maid's misfortune at last,
She sent for this young man she'd slighted with scorn,

She was pierced through the heart and did nothing but
    mourn.

"Well, good morning, pretty Sally, and how do you feel?
Is your pain in your head or is it in your heel?"
"O no, kind sir, the truth you have not guess'd,
For the pain that I feel pierces me through the breast."

"Well, am I a doctor, you sent for me so?
The truth of the story I mean for to know:"
"Oh! yes, kind sir, you can kill or can cure,
For without your assistance I'm ruined I'm sure."

"O Sally, O Sally, O Sally," said he,
"Oh, don't you remember how you slighted me?
I asked you a question, you answered with scorn,
And now I'll reward you for things past and gone."

"For things past and gone sir, I pray you'd forgive,
May Heaven permit me one day more to live."
"I ne'er will forgive you not while I have breath,
And I'll dance on your grave when your laid in the earth."

"Farewell to my parents, farewell to my friends,
Farewell to this young man, God make him amends,
For I can forgive him although he can't me,
For ten thousand times over my folly I see.

"Farewell to my friends, farewell to my foes,
Farewell to this troublesome world also;"
Then off of her fingers took diamond rings three,
Saying, "Wear these for my sake when you're dancing on me."

"O Sally, O Sally, O Sally," said he,
"Put your rings on your fingers and married we'll be;"
This couple were married, they married speedily,
And as happy a couple as ever you see.

C

Melody to a version of this ballad, traditional for many years in Bury, P. Q., Canada. Sung at Newbury, Vermont, August 15, 1905, by Rosanna J. Parker.

Phillips Barry, Collector

Structure: A B A B (or A A) (2,2,2,2); Rhythm C; Contour: each half an arc; Scale: hexachordal

t.c. F.

For mel. rel. see BES, 419 (not very close); DV, 605, No. 50 (I).

The Brown Girl

Index

(Figures in parentheses indicate the Child number)

294   INDEX

Geographical Index

CONNECTICUT

Mystic:	Miss Mary Geneva Rathburn, 250 H
Naugatuck:	Mrs. Edwin White, 277 K
Stafford Springs:	Mrs. Forest A. Elkins, 286 II
Warren:	Edward Richards, 277 J
West Cornwall:	Oscar Degreenia, 250 B, 278 R
Westford:	Miss Emily Josephine Chism, 286 F

MAINE

Howland:	Mrs. Sarah Lane, 278 P
Kingman:	Adam Morris, 285 G
Machias:	Maria Dix, 277 L
Rumford Center:	Mrs. Harriet Gott Murphy, 286 K
Searsport:	Mrs. Bertha J. Kneeland, 250 G, 285 B
Stacyville:	Fred Brackett, 250 I, 278 Q
	Hanford Hayes, 250 C, 272 B, 286 DD
	Jack McNally, 285 E
York:	Alonzo Lewis, 283 H
	Ralph Lewis, 287 B

MASSACHUSETTS

Boston:	Mrs. Silence Buck Bellows, 250 A
Brookline:	Mrs. Frances Kilbride, 275
Greenfield:	John A. Taggart, 278 S, 283 N, 286 N
New Bedford:	Mrs. Sarah Taylor, 289 C

NEW HAMPSHIRE

Source and name withheld—281	
Charlestown:	Orlon Merrill, 283 L
Colebrook:	Edwin Day, 283 C
	Mrs. Belle Richards, 250 D, 285 C, 286 Z
East Jaffrey:	Mrs. Lena Bourne Fish, 277 A, 285 D, 286 V
Hanover:	Mrs. Fred P. Lord, 283 F
Orford:	Jonathan Moses, 250 E, 278 G, 283 O, 286 M
	Mrs. Mabel Pease, 250 J, 277 I, 286 P